IDENTITY

T.D. JAKES

IDENTITY

DISCOVER WHO YOU ARE AND
LIVE A LIFE OF PURPOSE

WHERE YOUR **TRUE PURPOSE** IS REVEALED

© Copyright 2015–T. D. Jakes

All rights reserved. This book is protected by the copyright laws of the United States of America. This book may not be copied or reprinted for commercial gain or profit. The use of short quotations or occasional page copying for personal or group study is permitted and encouraged. Permission will be granted upon request. Unless otherwise identified, Scripture quotations are taken from the New King James Version. Copyright © 1982 by Thomas Nelson, Inc. Used by permission. All rights reserved. Scripture quotations marked NLT are taken from the Holy Bible, New Living Translation, copyright © 1996, 2004. Used by permission of Tyndale House Publishers, Wheaton, Illinois 60189. All rights reserved. Scripture quotations marked KJV are taken from the King James Version. Scripture quotations marked NIV are taken from the HOLY BIBLE, NEW INTERNATIONAL VERSION®, copyright © 1973, 1978, 1984, 2011 International Bible Society. Used by permission of Zondervan. All rights reserved. All emphasis within Scripture quotations is the author's own. Please note that Destiny Image's publishing style capitalizes certain pronouns in Scripture that refer to the Father, Son, and Holy Spirit, and may differ from some publishers' styles. Take note that the name satan and related names are not capitalized. We choose not to acknowledge him, even to the point of violating grammatical rules.

Previously published content from *When Power Meets Potential*

DESTINY IMAGE® PUBLISHERS, INC.
P. O. Box 310, Shippensburg, PA 17257-0310
"Promoting Inspired Lives"

This book and all other Destiny Image and Destiny Image fiction books are available at Christian bookstores and distributors worldwide.

For more information on foreign distributors, call 717-532-3040.

Reach us on the Internet: www.destinyimage.com.

ISBN 13 HC: 978-0-7684-1370-0
ISBN 13 TP: 978-0-7684-0808-9
ISBN 13 Ebook: 978-0-7684-0809-6

For Worldwide Distribution. Printed in the U.S.A.

2 3 4 5 6 7 8 / 18 17 16 15

Contents

Introduction 9

Chapter 1   You Are on Purpose 13

Chapter 2   Get Ready for Your Moment 29

Chapter 3   Experience the God of Purpose..... 45

Chapter 4   Elevate Your Understanding of Purpose.................... 67

Chapter 5   Find Your Place of Deposit....... 85

Chapter 6   Identifying Unrealized Potential... 105

Chapter 7   Unwrap the Gift of Exposure.... 123

Final Thoughts................ 137

BONUS MATERIALS

Faithing It! *by Cora Jakes-Coleman* 141

Introduction.................. 143

Chapter 1   You Are God's Book—Respect the Process................... 151

and a selection from

STRENGTH FOR EVERY MOMENT Devotional 171

INTRODUCTION

So many people are intensely searching for purpose and meaning in life. Maybe this describes where you are *right now*.

Are you asking questions like, *Why am I here? What have I been put on this planet to do? What is my destiny?* Here is the problem with how many people approach the question of purpose: many are looking outside of themselves for their purpose, destiny, or meaning in life. The very key to knowing your purpose is discovering and celebrating your personal identity.

When you know *who* you are, *how* you have been intricately designed by the Master Craftsman, and *discover* that you have been uniquely

IDENTITY

gifted to fulfill a divine calling, your eyes will cease wandering to and fro, ogling over the clothes Sally has or dreaming about having Jimmy's job or Mary's husband or Bobby's wife or Susan's house or Joe's country club membership. To fulfill your purpose, you must first know and celebrate your identity!

In the age of social media, it seems like now, more than ever, we are bombarded with images that constantly tell us: "The grass is greener over here." This is exactly why we want Sally's clothes or Jimmy's job.

What we *don't* realize is:

- Social media is like the "highlight reel," often exposing us only to the best of someone's life. You only see the ups and are rarely exposed to the downs or the humdrum normalcy of everyday life.
- Every moment spent envying another person is a moment spent living *outside* of your life purpose.

Introduction

God did not create you to be jealous of who someone else is or what they are doing; He created you uniquely to fulfill *your* destiny.

It's time to stop longing for what other people have and give up trying to be anyone other than *you*. Remember, as long as you invest your time trying to be someone else, or pursuing what others have, you are *not* being the person God created you to be.

In the journey ahead, I give you permission to *stop* looking at others' lives and quit longing for what they have. You are going to see from the example of one of the most powerful Old Testament prophets, Elisha, that your identity is *not* wrapped up in someone else—it's *distinctly yours!*

In the pages of *Identity,* you will first become reintroduced to the God of purpose—to know and experience Him like never before. You will also learn how to seize the destiny-defining moments that will advance you further into fulfilling your purpose.

You will discover why it is so important to invest your time, resources, and energies into good soil that will ultimately produce a harvest in your life; this is about finding your place of deposit!

Finally, you will receive a divine blueprint in the lives of Elijah and Elisha on how to step into the unique identity that God has crafted for you and discover your unrealized potential.

In the same way that Heaven had unique assignments for Elijah and Elisha, you have likewise been awarded a specific and strategic assignment that is absolutely exclusive to your life. No one else can fulfill it. No one else can carry it full term. No one else can steward and execute it quite like you. Others may try, but they will fail to grasp the glory that is reserved for you.

Discover who you are.

Celebrate your unique identity in Christ.

Fulfill your purpose and be the solution the world is waiting for.

CHAPTER 1

You Are on Purpose

For You formed my inward parts; You covered me in my mother's womb. I will praise You, for I am fearfully and wonderfully made; marvelous are Your works, and that my soul knows very well. My frame was not hidden from You, when I was made in secret, and skillfully wrought in the lowest parts of the earth. Your eyes saw my substance, being yet unformed. And in Your book they all were written, the days fashioned for me, when as yet there were none of them (Psalm 139:13-16).

For we are God's masterpiece. He has created us anew in Christ Jesus, so we can do the good things he planned for us long ago (Ephesians 2:10 NLT).

"For I know the plans I have for you," says the Lord. *"They are plans for good and not for disaster, to give you a future and a hope"* (Jeremiah 29:11 NLT).

YOU HAVE A PURPOSE

Your hands have made me and fashioned me… (Job 10:8).

- You have a purpose.
- You were created *on purpose*.
- You were formed, fashioned, and knit together by a skilled Craftsman, not by some arbitrary cosmic explosion.
- You are not an accident.
- You are not an incident.
- You are not a mistake.

- You are not just a glob of protoplasmic material that is the result of a reckless night or a weekend between two passionate lovers.
- You are not just a mere mixing together of DNA.

You have a divine purpose. You were allowed access into this dimension of life by the nod of the Creator Himself, that you would be strategically placed at this time, at this age, in your gender, in your ethnicity, with your gifting, and with your talent for God's divine purpose.

Even the wealthiest person on the planet could not offer up any suitable form of tender that could purchase *purpose*. Surely they wish purpose could have a dollar value assigned to it, because then the relentless nagging of their souls could be silenced. They could rest easy knowing that the one unknown of life has been secured. Purpose is priceless, while purposelessness is very costly.

You can live in this world and make all the money you could ever dream of and be as beautiful as you want and be as educated as you please and accomplish whatever you want to, but if you die without accomplishing your purpose, you are a failure, a reject, and a fool.

THE ROOT OF PURPOSELESSNESS

The fool has said in his heart, "There is no God" (Psalm 14:1).

The fool has said, "There is no God, there is no purpose, there is no meaning." He further adds, "I can do my own thing, go my own way, live my own life."

The fool who says in his heart, "There is no God" has essentially said, "There is no purpose." To divorce one's perspective from the reality of a Creator, a Master Designer, and a Purpose-Author, one is rejecting purpose and meaning as a whole. This is no small statement because it is no small action.

The repercussions of saying, *"There is no God"* are far-reaching into every arena of our lives and society. It is downright deadly to reject the reality of a Creator, for it is that very Creator who assigns value and purpose to the created. If the created is without a Creator, then who or what assigns value or purpose to the created? There are no constants. There's nothing certain. We are without anchors. No one knows who they are, because they are detached from the truth of *Whose* they are.

When Genesis 1 becomes a fairy tale and we are disconnected from the fact that we were created in the *"image and likeness of God"* (see Genesis 1:26), that we were in fact handcrafted in the image of the perfect Craftsman, purpose-*less*ness abounds. Now, more than ever, we need this vision of the Creator and created; for as the Scripture says, *"Where there is no vision, the people perish…"* (Proverbs 29:18 kjv).

The world perishes because of the purposelessness of its people; people perish because they

IDENTITY

live without vision. I want to invite you to consider the vision of your Creator.

> **The value of your Creator should cause you to reconsider your own worth and value.**

As mentioned earlier, you are not some type of cosmic accident. You were handcrafted and custom-made by a perfect Creator. The value of your Creator should cause you to reconsider your own worth and value. God did not make you in the image of an animal. He did not create you in the image of an angel. Rather, He created you in His very own image and likeness. Time after time, Scripture invites us to consider the unlikeness of God.

> *Who is like You, O Lord, among the gods?...* (Exodus 15:11).
>
> *"Lord God of Israel, there is no God in heaven or on earth like You..."* (2 Chronicles 6:14).

> *Who is like the Lord our God, who dwells on high* (Psalm 113:5).

Because God radically stands out and above everything and everyone else in created order, consider the precious value that someone created in *His* image and likeness carries. *That someone is you.*

GOD CREATED YOU UNIQUELY

> *Then God said, "Let Us make man in Our image, according to Our likeness…"* (Genesis 1:26).

Once you realize that you were created on purpose, and created in the image of the Creator, you begin to recognize that there are secrets stored up inside you. These are the very secrets that must be discovered and unleashed to a purposeless planet and a purposeless people.

There are secrets inside you that God has planted—secret talents, secret gifts, and secret wisdom—that have been divinely orchestrated.

IDENTITY

These gifts, talents, abilities, wisdom, solutions, and creativities are uniquely *yours*. God the Creator is multidimensional enough to create you uniquely. Trust His design. The moment you start to embrace how you have been formed and fashioned is the moment you step into the very purpose for which you were created.

God is not the author of prolonged purposelessness; you are. One of the most prevalent enemies to you stepping into your purpose is the downright deception that "the grass is greener." In other words, something in someone else causes you to reject and ultimately neglect the unique purpose within you. This keeps you exactly where the enemy wants you, and sadly, where the world cannot afford to keep you. You cannot make a difference sitting off in a dark corner somewhere, wishing that you were someone else.

Stop, stop, stop wanting to be somebody else. Do not insult your Creator by insulting His creation. You were fearfully and wonderfully made. Can you even fathom what the psalmist is expressing by using those words—*fearfully and wonderfully?* (See Psalm 139:14.) You were created with awe. God didn't just throw you together, stand back and say, "This looks good." Because God fashioned you in His very image and likeness, He has a right to stand back and actually awe His own creation. Why? It's simply God standing in awe of His own handiwork; God awing God. This is how He looks upon *you.*

In fact, God considers you a "masterpiece." (See Ephesians 2:10 NLT.) God made you the way He wanted to make you so He could use you at a particular time in a particular way; and if you start trying to be like somebody else, you're going to miss *your purpose.*

People don't miss their purpose and bypass destiny because God decides to take it away; they miss purpose because they fail to invest in *their* purpose. One of the greatest ways we fail to invest in what God has wired into OUR DNA is through rejecting who we have been uniquely created to be and what we have been created to bring to this moment in history.

YOU HAVE WHAT IT TAKES

His divine power has given to us all things that pertain to life and godliness... (2 Peter 1:3).

You have everything you need to do what you've been designed to do and be what you were created to be. I repeat, you have everything you need to accomplish your purpose. If God needed you to be tall, He would have made you tall. If He needed you to be better looking, He would have made you better looking. If He needed you to have a voice to sing, He would have given you a voice to sing. Everything about you was designed with intentionality. In fact, your design is directly connected to your purpose.

If you neglect your design and refuse to celebrate *how* you were made, you will never step into *who* you were made to be. We have no right to question the Potter about how He fashioned and molded the clay.

In Romans 9:20 NIV, Paul directly confronts this issue of questioning the Maker about how the creation was made. He writes,

> *But who are you, a human being, to talk back to God? "Shall what is formed say to the one who formed it, 'Why did You make me like this?'"*

God knew what He was doing when He created you like He did. He gave you the right IQ and He gave you the right personality. He gave you the right temperament. Do not despise your design, for the Designer made you a certain way so that you could accomplish a certain purpose.

Like I said, the more you disregard your design and continue to want to be like someone else, the more you distance yourself from stepping into your created purpose. You, *as you are,* have got what it takes to *be* who God has created you to be. Yes, get educated. Yes, get equipped and trained. Yes, pursue knowledge, learning, and wisdom. Scripture tells us to pursue these things, as anyone can have as much of these things as he or she desires. Just don't despise who God has created *you* to be.

> *The Designer made you a certain way so that you could accomplish a certain purpose.*

Start believing this. You won't need as much counseling. You won't need as much therapy. You won't be as intimidated by other people. You won't be jealous of other people. If you understand your purpose, you will live in that purpose, and you will discover your gifts and your talents and what you were put here to do.

DEALING WITH THE LIE

> *Lead me by Your truth and teach me, for You are the God who saves me. All day long I put my hope in You* (Psalm 25:5 NLT).

And finally, whatever you've been through and whatever weaknesses you have, and whatever issues you've had—do not allow those weaknesses to abort your mission. Everyone has failed. Everyone has messed up. Everyone has slipped, fallen, gotten up, fallen again, gotten up again, maybe wandered around in the dark for a season, or moved on.

The devil is a liar, and he would love to deceive you right out of your destiny. One of the main tools he uses is reminding you of issues, hang-ups, setbacks, and sins. Your comeback should trump his lies *every* time. Your past is under the blood of Jesus. Your sins were dealt with at Calvary. God is not surprised by your weaknesses; this is why He promises strength! God is not caught off guard by your setbacks and problems.

> **It's never too late to get back on the path to purpose.**

IDENTITY

Remember, it's not your weaknesses and failures that have the potential to abort your mission; it's how you see and respond to them. If you believe your weaknesses can abort your purpose, you will live in agreement with that lie. Nothing—absolutely nothing—can separate you from God's purpose for your life *unless* you start agreeing with lies. It's this type of agreement that causes you to veer off the path God has set for you. If you've been believing these lies, I encourage you to start disagreeing with the liar *today*. It's never too late to get back on the path to purpose.

I repeat—you have a divine mission to accomplish. You cannot allow *anything* to come between you and your purpose.

In the pages ahead, we are going to look at the unique exchange that took place between Elijah and Elisha. As Elijah's time on earth was concluding, it was Elisha's turn to step up. If you need an example of someone who refused to let anything come between him and his purpose, this plowman turned prophet is your model. In fact, he is your mandate.

I'm calling for a company of Elishas to rise up in this hour, recognize their moment of visitation, and start running toward the divine purpose God has ready to release through their lives.

Reflection Questions

1. In what ways is your design (how you were made) directly connected to fulfilling your purpose in life?
2. Why is it an insult to the Creator to question the way He made you?
3. How can your weaknesses and failures keep you from fulfilling your purpose?

CHAPTER 2

Get Ready for Your Moment

So he departed from there, and found Elisha the son of Shaphat, who was plowing with twelve yoke of oxen before him... (1 Kings 19:19).

PREPARE FOR YOUR DESTINY-DEFINING MOMENT

Now we set out upon the journey to unlocking purpose. The first key to unlocking your purpose is preparing for destiny-defining moments. Be watchful, steadfast, and alert!

IDENTITY

It's in these moments when power meets potential, the power of God connects with the potential within you, and you are supernaturally catapulted into the predestined, preordained purpose that God has assigned to your life.

Throughout this book, we will be looking at the account of Elijah and Elisha and how their relationship is an example of what happens when you discover your identity and purpose. For Elisha, it began with a *moment*. For you, it will be the same way. To step into your divine purpose, you need to recognize and steward your divine moments.

In this chapter, I want us to look at how Elisha responded to his moment of visitation. This gives us a powerful picture of how to respond when your moment walks up to you.

It begins in First Kings 19:19:

> *So he departed from there, and found Elisha the son of Shaphat, who was*

plowing with twelve yoke of oxen before him, and he was with the twelfth. Then Elijah passed by him and threw his mantle on him.

Based on the text in First Kings 19, I want to share some vital keys to recognizing and stewarding your destiny-defining moments.

DESTINY-DEFINING MOMENTS HAPPEN QUICKLY

Then Elijah passed by him and threw his mantle on him (1 Kings 19:19b).

First of all, notice how quickly Elisha's moment happened. While Elisha was plowing, Elijah the prophet passed by and *threw his mantle on him*. There was no ceremony or service. They did not sit down over a business lunch and discuss the logistics of what the mantle transference process would look and function like. There was no red tape. There were no e-mails. There were no phone conferences, Skype conversations, or cross-country travel reservations. Elisha was plowing, and Elijah—representative of Elisha's divine moment—*passed by him* and tossed the mantle upon him.

I know this example will probably mess up some people's thoughts. That's good. I want to mess you up, because it's in the process of messing you up when the Holy Spirit renews your mind. He's cleaning up your thinking and enabling you to accommodate His supernatural ways and workings.

You see, I want to mess up your expectations of how you've got it planned out. So many of us are in bondage to preconceived ideas of how we assume God should launch us into our purpose and destiny. If your mind can comfortably wrap itself around a scenario, most likely the Holy Spirit is going to uncomfortably remove the wrapping and invite you into an elevated perspective.

The main problem with our planning is that it discounts the power of moments—*quick moments*. Planning usually involves the image of a process. We consider the ideal process of how some certain result should come to pass. I say it again, God wants to radically mess up your process. This doesn't mean you stop thinking, cease dreaming, and quit planning. There is a difference between having a plan and being in bondage to your plan.

Have a plan. Have a dream. Have goals. Have expectations. Have processes. Have a picture. Have an image. Have these things, but don't become yoked to them. Don't dare exalt your plan over the power of a God-ordained, destiny-defining moment. One divine moment orchestrated by the Master can shift things that have taken you a lifetime to change.

> **One divine moment orchestrated by the Master can shift things that have taken you a lifetime to change.**

IDENTITY

Going back to First Kings 19:19, it appears that Elisha's moment could have taken place in the blink of an eye. One moment he was plowing with twelve yoke of oxen; the next, he receives an invitation in the form of a mantle that would radically shift his destiny.

The same is true for you. Your day of visitation is at hand. Your moment is waiting for you to be ready. Don't start getting paranoid, trying to figure out what your moment should look like. Elisha had no clue that his moment would look like some prophet throwing a mantle on him. In fact, it seems like Elisha recognized his moment "after the fact." It was only after the mantle had fallen upon him and Elijah passed by that Elisha turned and ran after the prophet. Even if he was a minute behind his moment, he nevertheless recognized the power of his moment and responded appropriately.

Your key to being ready to run when your moment of visitation comes is simple. More than focusing on a moment, keep your eyes fixed on the Master. When the mantle hits, it is the still small voice of the Holy Spirit that will say, "This is your moment, son. This is your time, daughter. *Get running!*" We need to always be in a state of readiness and expectation, as we never know when those moments will happen when God's power collides with our potential.

DESTINY-DEFINING MOMENTS TAKE PLACE IN THE ORDINARY AND EVERYDAY

> *So he departed from there, and found Elisha the son of Shaphat, who was plowing with twelve yoke of oxen before him, and he was with the twelfth...* (1 Kings 19:19a).

Second, it is important to understand that destiny-defining moments take place in ordinary, everyday circumstances. In order to be trusted with a destiny-defining moment, we need to be good stewards of the unique moment we have been given *right now*.

Consider Elisha. He was simply being a good steward of where he was at his unique moment in history. He used his moments well, thus enabling him to be trusted with *the* moment. How we spend the sum of our everyday moments determines how we will respond to those life-altering, destiny-defining moments that come.

I want to unpack this more, as I believe the secret to increase in the Kingdom has everything to do with stewarding what you have. How you handle the everyday shows God how you can be trusted with the extraordinary. Jesus notes this in His parable of the talents. The steward who was faithful receives this verbal recognition from his lord, *"Well done, good and faithful servant; you have been faithful over a few things, I will make you ruler over many things…"* (Matthew 25:23). The "few things" for Elisha was his plowing. What are these "few things" for you?

> *How you handle the everyday shows God how you can be trusted with the extraordinary.*

When Elijah approached Elisha, the setting was nothing above average. There weren't heavenly beams and angelic choirs singing. Scripture tells us that Elisha was participating in something very common at the time. He was diligently plowing with the twelve yoke of oxen that were *before him*—the thing that was under his charge. He was faithful with what was before him, and this faithfulness positioned him to be in the right place at the right time when his moment came.

Too many of us want to chase after a destiny-defining moment; and as a result, we spend our entire lives running after something that should be running alongside us, ready to collide with our path. *Destiny-defining moments are like magnets to people who used their everyday moments well.* Do not despise where you are. Do not look negatively upon small beginnings. You are where you are for a reason, just like Elisha was exactly where he was for a reason—for that moment.

Also, too many desire a moment without recognizing that it is the sum of everyday moments that prepares a person to receive and run after their *moment*. Again, this should bring peace to our minds, which tend to fret over how and when our moment will come.

This might sound backward, but the truth is that those who become obsessed with seeking out *their moment* are actually ill-prepared for it and have the propensity to miss it when it presents itself. Why? God is looking for good stewards to trust with His greater works. He is looking for those who appropriately steward the life they have been given before He promotes them into greater levels of glory, anointing, and power.

Many people seek after promotion from the usual, when in fact, God withholds the very thing they seek. He does not do this out of denial, but rather out of protection. Listen, God will protect you *from* your own promotion if that promotion has the potential to destroy you, or if you're not ready for it.

It's no mystery. Those who are faithful with the moments they have been given are positioning themselves for greater promotion; while those striving after promotion, but are neglecting the moments in front of them, are being spared from a tragic downfall.

Keep in mind, it's everyday moments that prepare everyday people for extraordinary exploits. Character is developed in the moments. Integrity is cultivated in the moments. The fruit of the Spirit grow in the moments. Christlikeness, godliness, and holiness are birthed in the moments. God is examining your moments, for they gauge your preparedness for *the moment*.

DESTINY-DEFINING MOMENTS DEMAND A RAPID RESPONSE

And he left the oxen and ran after Elijah... (1 Kings 19:20).

The first thing we looked at was the swiftness of a moment's arrival. Scripture reminds us that *"Elijah passed by him* [Elisha] *and threw his mantle on him"* (1 Kings 19:19b). A quick moment demands an equally rapid response.

Before I continue, I want you to know that this is not some call to run after everything and make hasty decisions. There is balance. Elisha, no doubt, recognized that his moment was God-birthed and God-ordained.

Before changing your life, switching jobs, moving across the country, marrying that guy, dating that girl, or doing something radical, the most important rapid, radical responses must always be to the One who authors your moment.

Let your heart be like Abraham's in Genesis 22, where he is brought into a destiny-defining moment. God instructs Abraham to sacrifice his son, Isaac, giving him up as a burnt offering before the Lord. Pay careful attention to how the scenario plays out. Before Abraham took his son up the mountain, prepared the altar, and yes, even raised the knife over the boy—only to be supernaturally stopped by the Angel of the Lord—Abraham offered a rapid response to God by saying "Yes" to His divine instruction. God set up the moment, and *"Abraham rose early in the morning and saddled his donkey, and took two of his young men with him, and Isaac his son; and he split the wood for the burnt offering, and arose and went to the place of which God had told him"* (Genesis 22:3).

> *Our rapid response always belongs to God first.*

Our rapid response always belongs to God first. He will reveal the specifics. He will provide direction. His Spirit will lead us and guide us. In order to position ourselves for divine guidance, we must offer a rapid, definitive "Yes" to what God is asking of us.

Abraham did not wait around, giving himself time to talk himself out of the difficult thing God was asking him to do. God gave Abraham instruction, and we notice that *"Abraham rose early in the morning"* to begin this journey. He didn't wait around, pacing the floor, giving himself the opportunity to consider some other, user-friendly options. First thing in the morning, Abraham got up and began walking toward a moment that would not only define his life, but a prophetic moment that would set up history for *the moment* that would change everything. That moment would be the Cross of Calvary.

How did Elisha respond to his destiny-defining moment? *"And he left the oxen and ran after Elijah..."* (1 Kings 19:20). Moments happen *that* fast.

In future chapters, I want us to look at *why* these moments are so powerful and how they unlock the potential inside of you. For now, we know that any God-orchestrated moment is worthy of our rapid response. Our "Yes" to God prepares us to say "Yes" to every decision we need to make in order to embrace the moment that is being presented to us. Likewise, our "Yes" to God emboldens us to say "No" to everything that would try to restrain us from promotion.

Previously, we considered people who were ill-prepared for promotion. Just as bad as those who receive promotion who are not prepared for it are those who *are ready* for promotion, but don't recognize its life-changing invitation that demands their response. Run after it like Elisha did.

When your moment arrives, all bets are off. Running after a moment cannot produce that divine moment in your life. However, running toward a moment, *when the moment presents itself,* will bring your life into alignment with the power of that moment, and ultimately, God's glorious purpose for your life.

IDENTITY

 **Reflection Questions**

1. What do you think a destiny-defining moment looks like for you? What did it look like for Elisha?

2. What are the three characteristics of destiny-defining moments—and how should you respond to them?

3. What is the difference between running *after* a moment and running *toward* a moment?

CHAPTER 3

Experience the God of Purpose

There he went into a cave, and spent the night in that place; and behold, the word of the Lord came to him, and He said to him, "What are you doing here, Elijah?" (1 Kings 19:9).

And we know that all things work together for good to those who love God, to those who are the called according to His purpose (Romans 8:28).

For in him we live and move and have our being… (Acts 17:28 NIV).

IDENTITY

KNOW THE GOD OF PURPOSE

In Him we were also chosen, having been predestined according to the plan of Him who works out everything in conformity with the purpose of His will (Ephesians 1:11 NIV).

It is by God's divine purpose that power and potential intersect and meet. It is a mystery that I think is worth discussing. First things first. You need to know that the God you serve is a strategic God. He is the God of absolute purpose. He is the God who has a strategy, and according to Ephesians 1:11 KJV, He *"worketh all things after the counsel of His own will."*

> **The God you serve is a strategic God–the God of absolute purpose.**

Nothing "just happened." Creation was not arbitrary. There are no cosmic blunders or mishaps. The God who created you is the same

God who brought order to chaos, form to the formless, and purpose to nothingness. You may feel like that. You might feel like your life is formless, your future looks void of hope, and you have no purpose. Remind yourself, you were created by a God of Purpose. Nothing He made was created by accident—it was all sculpted with great skill and precision.

It was according to God's preordained purpose and divine design that He brought you into the world—and ultimately saved your soul. It was not your distress signal that brought God into your life. It was God who brought the distress signal that made you cry out after Him. Think about it. God is not just responding to your cry. He actually put the cry deep down inside you. He has put *eternity in your heart* (see Ecclesiastes 3:11). He designed you in such a way that only He could satisfy the deep void inside your heart (see Psalm 42:7). In fact, the deep that *calls unto deep* was placed inside you by God Himself. He made it possible for you to even have a deep that could cry out to the deep of Himself.

God is not responding to you seeking Him. He put the seek down in you. This didn't just happen. You didn't just happen. God has a unique purpose and an essential role for you to play, and He's working everything, good or bad, in your life after the counsel of His own will. This should bring us great relief and freedom.

Before we spend additional time studying how *our* potential is released and how we fulfill *our* purpose, it is foundational that we become acquainted with the God of Purpose. If we are confident in His nature as the One who is strategic and purposeful in all that He does, it will become much easier to trust that everything is in His most capable hands.

TRUST THE GOD OF PURPOSE

For the Word of the Lord holds true, and we can trust everything He does (Psalm 33:4 NLT).

In view of this reality about God's purposeful character, we really ought to just stop the murmuring and complaining and sit back and let Him drive. Trust Him! His Word holds true, and everything He says and everything He does can be trusted. He knows what He's doing. He will bring into your life who He wants to bring into your life. Conversely, He will bring out of your life who He wants to bring out of your life.

> **Nothing any human being says or does can restrain God's purpose from coming to pass in your life.**

He has a purpose and a strategy that defies human comprehension; and though many people don't understand why you are in the position or the role or the place you are in life, haters cannot stop your destiny. Their words, their slander, their accusations, their antagonisms, their doubts, their mockeries, their jokes—nothing any human being says or does can restrain God's purpose from coming to pass in your life.

Consider the timeless accounts in Scripture of men and women persevering through their odds and experiencing their destiny. Mockers could not keep Noah from building an ark and saving the world. Egyptian armies could not keep Israel from leaving bondage and crossing the Red Sea. Insults could not keep Hannah from believing for her son. An insult-hurling giant could not keep David from securing a supernatural victory over the Philistine army. Persecution could not keep the Gospel of Jesus Christ from spreading throughout the known world. The seed of each monumental victory was everyday people trusting the God of Purpose in spite of what everything and everyone else was saying or doing.

Your job? Continue to agree with the God of Purpose. Remember, the enemy wants you to bow down to his lies. These lies come in the different forms we just looked at. He uses words. He uses memories. He uses something a parent said, something a teacher said, something a peer or student or co-worker said to try and deceive you right out of your destiny. Trust the God of Purpose, for the same God who is full of purpose is also full of power. He is also entirely sovereign.

This means that He will make sure that your purpose is fulfilled, regardless of what people say, regardless of what problems come, and regardless of how certain seasons of life treat you. Keep trusting the God of Purpose. The One who brings you *through* will also bring you *to*.

THE ENEMY OF YOUR PURPOSE

The thief comes only to steal and kill and destroy... (John 10:10 NIV).

Keep in mind, your purpose has an adversary (see 1 Peter 5:8). This adversary, the devil, recruits a number of different methods of antagonism. These are the assignments aimed directly at your purpose. All of the mean things

IDENTITY

people have said, all of the mean things that they do, and all of the things that they set out against you are weapons of the adversary, targeted at your purpose.

Stand on the truth that *"No weapon that is formed against thee shall prosper..."* (Isaiah 54:17 KJV). No weapon that the enemy aims at your purpose can dismantle it or defuse it. Why? Because God is going to see your purpose through to completion. The One who *"began a good work in you will carry it on to completion until the day of Christ Jesus"* (Philippians 1:6 NIV). God's purpose for your life *will* come to pass.

> **No weapon that the enemy aims at your purpose can dismantle it or defuse it.**

Remember, satan is merely trying to steer you off course. He can't destroy your purpose. He also knows that you can't just lose your purpose, like someone loses a sock in the dryer or their car keys in the sofa. He knows that his only formidable weapon against your purpose is securing your allegiance with his deception. When you start believing his lies over the truth of the God of Purpose, the devil begins to unleash his assault against your purpose. Again, it's not his tactics, tools, or terrorism that have any prevailing power against your purpose. What positions us for defeat is actually believing the enemy is more of a threat than he really is.

One of his main targets is your identity. He challenges your worthiness to fulfill God's purpose by using people to attack you. All of the lies and the spirit behind the lies that are sent out against you, these are the enemy's attempts to distract you from purpose.

The more you contemplate the negative things people are speaking against you, the less time you have to consider the greatness of the God of Purpose. He will surely bring His plans to fruition in your life and complete the good work He began.

Your adversary knows that by getting people to spread lies and rumors and falsehoods about you, he is able to get you in that corner of distraction. It's like you are in the corner of a room, staring at a wall that is papered in lies. The lies try to consume your view, while God's truth is waiting just behind you, beckoning your refocus.

If the enemy cannot distract you with lies, he will even try to use truth against you. He's desperate to distract you right out of stepping into your purpose by keeping your eyes off the God of Purpose. If you successfully stand your ground during his barrage of lies, the serpent will attempt another strategy. You see, the devil is an expert at digging up the dirt of your past and doing whatever he can to get you to stare at it—apart from the blood of Jesus. The Bible identifies satan as the *"accuser of our brethren"* (Revelation 12:10). You are his target, not God. He cannot accuse you before God because of the *"better things"* that Jesus' blood speaks

(Hebrews 12:24), but he knows that he can try to deceive believers right out of their status in Christ.

My goal here is not to make us overly conscious of the devil. Yet to defeat him and overcome his schemes, we must be aware of his tactics. Paul makes this clear, indicating that if we are ignorant of the enemy's devices, we can fall prey easily to his schemes (see 2 Corinthians 2:11).

One of the enemy's greatest lies concerning your purpose is that *you are unworthy to step into so great a purpose.* We just discussed the fact that he delights in trying to veer you off course by reminding you of your past, your sins, your setbacks, your failures, your issues, your obstacles, your bondages, your addictions, etc.

Here's the truth—the God of Purpose will walk with you through each of these. He brings hope, healing, forgiveness, cleansing, deliverance, freedom—every solution to every obstacle.

IDENTITY

Listen to me. It's not the obstacle or the failure that keeps us from pursuing purpose; it's what we believe about the *power* of the obstacles that keeps us in limbo. This is where the enemy works overtime, trying to convince us that our stuff has the ability to keep us from stepping into divine purpose. This is a flat out lie. Sin, hell, and death itself cannot prevent Almighty God from reaching down into your mess, invading your life, cleansing you with Jesus's blood, filling you with the Holy Spirit, and setting you on a course for victory.

Just think about it. If death could not keep you from stepping into God's divine plan and design for your life, what could possibly hold you back? God has dealt with every possible barrier. However, there is one you will deal with throughout your life and you must learn to confront if you desire to walk into your destiny. This is the boundary of belief. What do you believe about your identity and your purpose to fulfill it? Don't let the devil distract you.

THE GOD OF PURPOSE USES YOU IN SPITE OF YOURSELF

And He said to me, "My grace is sufficient for you, for My strength is made perfect in weakness." Therefore most gladly I will rather boast in my infirmities, that the power of Christ may rest upon me (2 Corinthians 12:9).

We need to stop focusing on ourselves so much. God does not use us because of us; He uses us *in spite of us.* Paul the apostle recognized this on several dimensions. He had weaknesses that should have disqualified him from ministry. These were not restrictive, though. God used Paul in spite of his weaknesses, and He will use you in the same way.

Remember, it is not because of you that God chose you; it is because of His divine purpose. Just think about it for a moment. Why in the world would God use David to be a king? He had no background of a king, he was not trained as a king, he didn't live in the palace, and he was not reared up in an environment of kingly order. He was a shepherd boy, a goat chaser, and yet God said, *"I have found…a man after My own heart"* (see Acts 13:22).

> *It is not because of you that God chose you; it is because of His divine purpose.*

Did that mean that David was perfect, or even close to being perfect? Absolutely not. And it doesn't just mean that David was a God-seeker, though he definitely fit that mold. Truly, God looked upon young David and declared, *I have found the man who is after My heart, who is after My purpose, who fits the spot of My purpose and destiny. I have found him. He's out there in the wilderness. He fits right into the strategic purpose of what I have orchestrated, and I will use him in spite of himself.*

Now you can sit there, read these words, and act like you don't understand that, but if you have walked with God at all, you have come to discover that God uses you in spite of you—not because of you! In fact, the conditions that seem to make you the least likely candidate for a God-sized destiny are the very factors that maintain your humility.

The devil is trying to use our own weapons against us. We need to know that our past is not a weapon against us, but an anchor—a pillar. Our past, our surroundings, and our upbringing remind us where we came from, that God stepped in and chose us in spite of ourselves.

Once when I was being interviewed, the reporter noted that I exhibited a humility that did not match my circumstances, and then proceeded to ask me, "How do you stay humble, Bishop Jakes?" Here's my answer. I said, "Because I know me. I have no choice but to be humble. It is by God's grace that I stand where I stand. He uses me in spite of me. There are things that pulled me out of my comfort zone, that pulled me out of my insecurities and out of my inhibitions. *He* pulled me. I had no choice but to come. I didn't come because I was wonderful or better or perfect or superior or anything else. I came because He drew me by His right hand. He stretched forth His hand and said, *'I call you unto Myself, and I'm going to use you right there.'*" And the same is true for you!

YOUR PIECE IN THE PUZZLE

Though the Lord is great, He cares for the humble... (Psalm 138:6 NLT).

You'll never find your place until you find your purpose and you understand how we all fit together in the grand scheme of things.

Remember, God is the One who assigns your greater significance. You may not see it. You may not comprehend it. It might not compute with your natural mind, but you have to trust the God of Purpose. He has a master plan to assemble the pieces together in such a way that from His divine vantage point everything fits together, everything makes sense, and there is a perfect image of all the parts working together as a whole.

I repeat, in order to embrace the greater significance, you must trust the God of Purpose and not attempt to try to do His work for Him. He is the only One capable of putting this great jigsaw puzzle of purpose together. In order to fit in, you need to humble yourself before God and His purpose.

Think of it this way. Everything fits together like a jigsaw puzzle. Have you ever tried to sit down and put one of those things together? I'm not good at those puzzles because I don't have the patience. It takes order. It takes time. It takes meticulous observation and precision on behalf of the assembler to fit one like piece with its corresponding part.

With me, I want the stuff to fall into place *when I say so.* And so when I start working with those puzzles, I get angry. I get mad because there are too many of those little bitty pieces to

IDENTITY

be running around there. You know how it goes when you are trying to put one of those things together. One of the pieces either fell down behind the couch and you can't find it, or someone walked off with one in a pocket, and the entire project goes on hold because of the gaping hole in the puzzle.

I get no joy out of putting puzzles together. The process gets on my nerves. My patience is not suitable for the puzzle process. Because of this, I try to improvise. This is where so many of us stray from safety when it comes to walking down the path of purpose. We step into uncertain territory because of our unwillingness to wait on the Master Builder's divine timing and precision, and we start trying to make things fit together.

You know you've tried it. When one of those puzzles gets on my nerves and I can't find the missing piece—or the right piece—I'll take a piece that's *close* to fitting and I'll try to jam it down into the spot because it's so close to fitting. But it doesn't work out. Even though it looks very similar to the right piece, it is still the wrong piece. In trying to make a wrong piece fit, you have to tear out something to make it become something that it is not in order to fit into the place that it really doesn't fit.

Did you catch that? You need to celebrate who the Master Craftsman has created you to be, and not try to distort or disfigure yourself in trying to bring your purpose to pass the way *you* assume it should take place. Yes, there are growth areas. Of course we learn, grow, change, and develop. I'm not talking about that. I'm talking about who you are as the integral piece to God's glorious puzzle. I'm talking about how you have been uniquely designed, intricately wired, and purposefully positioned.

Don't try to become someone else in order to fulfill your purpose. Why? As long as you strive to be someone you're not, you will never fulfill *your* purpose.

IDENTITY

> *As long as you strive to be someone you're not, you will never fulfill your purpose.*

Remember, when you attempt to malign God's design by fitting yourself into a scheme or scenario where you don't fit, you have to tear something in who you are. What happens when you tear, or change yourself, to try and become someone else in hopes of trying to fit somewhere that you don't actually belong? Your little plan actually messes up the bigger picture of what you're trying to do, which is to ultimately fulfill purpose. I repeat, the longer you tear yourself by trying to become someone else, the longer you will prolong your journey toward purpose.

God curved you where you needed to be curved, made you straight where you needed to be straight, made you blue where you needed to be blue, yellow where you needed to be yellow, and as soon as you find that place where you fit...*purpose happens.*

Reflection Questions

1. How does the enemy try to distract you from your purpose?

2. What does it mean that God uses you *in spite of yourself?*

3. What can happen if you try to bring your purpose to pass *yourself* instead of waiting on God's divine timing?

CHAPTER 4

Elevate Your Understanding of Purpose

Now when David had served God's purpose in his own generation, he fell asleep; he was buried with his ancestors and his body decayed. (Acts 13:36 niv).

One generation shall praise Your works to another, and shall declare Your mighty acts (Psalm 145:4).

YOUR POSITION IN GOD'S DIVINE PROCESS

Once we recognize that God is orchestrating a master jigsaw puzzle, we begin to live our lives very differently. Why? Because no moment is arbitrary. Randomness is not part of the equation. We don't just wake up to sleepwalk through our day, only to come home, go to bed, wake up, and start the process all over again.

God is elevating your perspective concerning your purpose, for there are seeds of fulfilling your purpose in every waking moment. With every moment comes greater understanding of your unfolding purpose. You walk with a speaking God. This is your glory—that you know Him, and, yes, understand His unfolding plan of piecing the puzzle together. I want us to study the process through which God begins putting the puzzle together. This intersection is where power collides with potential and pushes us toward purpose.

First, understand that there is a divine process for putting the puzzle together.

In the beginning was the Word, and the Word was with God, and the Word was

God. He was in the beginning with God (John 1:1-2).

The Word is the logos. In the beginning, we see that the logos was with God, and the logos was God. The logos in the beginning was the strategy, and the strategy was with God and the strategy was God; and on account of His divine strategy, He pulls you in to fit a particular place and time and destiny. He then calls you to meet who you need to meet right when you need to meet them to draw the picture, and assemble the jigsaw puzzle of His purpose in the earth.

Our God is the Master Strategist. Everything He does brims with intentionality. God is not the author of coincidence; He is the sculptor of divine providence.

God is not the author of coincidence; He is the sculptor of divine providence.

IDENTITY

You must keep your eyes on God's divine strategy. If you don't, you run the risk of adopting the Elijah perspective. Even though we are studying the transference that took place between Elijah and *Elisha*, during Elijah's final golden days on earth, this prophet of power experienced some deep moments of despair. Why? He redirected his vision away from his purpose.

THE GREATER PICTURE OF PURPOSE

> *But he himself went a day's journey into the wilderness, and came and sat down under a broom tree. And he prayed that he might die, and said, "It is enough! Now, Lord, take my life, for I am no better than my fathers!"* (1 Kings 19:4)

Why did Elijah want to die here? Because something was missing, and he could not figure out what it was. His pain starts pointing him toward his purpose. At this point in the story, he has gone as far as he can go without meeting Elisha.

Elevate Your Understanding of Purpose

It is in this same chapter, First Kings 19, where Elijah experiences some of his darkest moments, as well as his finest hour. One would think that the prophet's finest hour preceded this chapter, when he called down fire from Heaven, experienced a miraculous demonstration of the power of God, and executed the false prophets of Baal. God used him to dramatically impact the spiritual landscape of an entire region, all in a single scene. And yet in the following chapter, we see the same man who experienced an overwhelming victory suffer under overwhelming depression. How was this possible?

> **Some moments that *appear* the most suited for purpose can actually distract you from fulfilling your purpose.**

As incredible as the victory at Mount Carmel was, that was not the moment where power would meet potential. Don't be deceived. Some moments that appear the most suited for purpose can actually distract you from fulfilling your purpose. Don't settle on a high. Celebrate breakthrough and victory, but don't mistakenly assume that a single demonstration of God's power *is* your purpose coming to pass. Rather, it serves as a landmark on your road to fulfilling your ultimate purpose.

There was a greater picture of purpose in Elijah's life than simply experiencing a significant victory against the prophets of Baal on Mount Carmel. It would have been easy for Elijah to mistakenly assume that a victory of that size was, in fact, the fulfillment of his purpose on earth. Perhaps he did entertain such a thought process. However, when we settle for small when God has greater, the ache and groan in our spirits will begin to push us outside of our wildernesses.

Elijah was not only in a wilderness physically, he was also in a wilderness mentally. Elijah's life purpose was not fulfilled in simply calling down fire from Heaven and destroying the false prophets of Baal. Likewise, your purpose is not fulfilled through some notable exploit you perform, a mighty act, or some type of spectacular feat. Even though these are God-ordained and God-orchestrated, they are moments that ultimately fade. Displays of power are fleeting, but transferences of power *awaken* potential in others. This is what Elijah was waiting for; he just didn't see it at the time.

Remember, God's vantage point includes so much more than human eyes are capable of capturing. It's tempting to coast on yesterday's victory, when in fact, God has bigger prepared. He is the God of *Greater Works*. I repeat, God has better. His vision is not for something fleeting or forgettable, but rather something sustained supernaturally. This is what He was preparing Elijah for, and yes, even used some of the prophet's pain to position him to anoint his successor, Elisha.

IDENTITY

THE MULTIDIMENSIONAL NATURE OF YOUR PURPOSE

"For My thoughts are not your thoughts, nor are your ways My ways," says the Lord (Isaiah 55:8).

Your Mount Carmel victory should not be unscalable. Why? Because your purpose is not wrapped up in a singular event; rather, it's your active participation in an unfolding, lifelong process. There are landmarks along the journey, but we cannot confuse a landmark for ultimate fulfillment. Perhaps Elijah considered his fiery victory as ultimate purpose fulfillment, when in fact, it was a piece of Heaven's divine jigsaw puzzle.

Our problem is that we often mistake great victories for the entire puzzle, and then become disappointed when another major victory is not waiting in the wings to continue that momentum.

We start redefining our purpose, not by the divine orchestration of God's unfolding plan, but rather by the size and scope of our victories, miracles, and blessings. Remember, these are all integral, essential parts of the journey. However, when we assume that *part* of the journey has become the *whole* journey, we position ourselves to live perpetually disappointed. The very object of our purpose is reduced to something that happened in the past. Right after your breakthrough comes and right on the other side of your miracle is an ominous future.

Consider it for a moment. What happens when we believe that our best days and greater victories are behind us, not before us? We cease pushing forward, for we see no potential in forward momentum. That's the danger of believing that purpose is fulfilled in an event or a landmark moment. There is far more to your purpose on earth than one breakthrough or miracle, no matter how spectacular or significant it appears to be.

It's like believing that a piece of the puzzle is the entire puzzle. And yet, God in His mercy gives us vision to see that the puzzle piece has interconnected edges longing for a complement. And you know that complement longs for a complementary piece, and so on and so forth. This is why I believe the puzzle analogy is most helpful in recognizing the flow and unfolding of God's purpose in our lives.

> *There is far more to your purpose on earth than one breakthrough or miracle.*

In other words, if we assume that a single victory or a significant event in our lives marks the complete fulfillment of our divine purpose, God is quick to remind us that what we assume is the whole is only a part. An essential part, yes, but still only a part. He gives us eyes to see the protruding edges on the pieces that are meant to connect and link with other pieces. He gives us the ability to see that what we perceive to be the be-all and end-all actually has missing portions.

You know how a puzzle piece has missing ends and edges, purposed to be complemented by a corresponding piece? In the same way, your breakthrough has missing portions. Whatever it is—a breakthrough, a blessing, a miracle, a victory, a promotion, an increase—God's purpose is higher and bigger. One event is merely one piece of your puzzle of purpose. One victory helps complete the puzzle, but is inadequate to masquerade as the entire image.

Make no mistake, events launch us into purpose. Breakthroughs escort us from one level to the next. Miracles override natural law, and position us in places that we could not have gotten to by ourselves. We celebrate moments without mistaking them for the ultimate masterpiece of God's divine design. We steward every significant event that takes place as a push that takes us from one dimension to the next, one realm of glory to another. We don't camp out at Carmel. We don't build a monument to every miracle—even the outstanding ones. Even the ones where fire falls down. We don't pitch a tent and try to live in yesterday, when in fact today is standing before us and we gaze, without purpose, into an uncertain future. Instead, we must see the catalysts for what they are and embrace their ability to move us along God's route for our lives.

THE MULTIGENERATIONAL NATURE OF YOUR PURPOSE

> *For I will pour water on him who is thirsty, and floods on the dry ground; I will pour My Spirit on your descendants, and My blessing on your offspring* (Isaiah 44:3).

In the same way assuming that a single significant event could capture the fulfillment of our purpose, we severely limit the expression of purpose when we simply focus on one person or a single generation. Purpose is beyond you, and it is beyond me. It is beyond our big breaks. It is beyond our successes. It is beyond our breakthroughs. It is beyond our victories.

In the same way that purpose was beyond Elijah, so the expression and fulfillment of purpose is beyond a single generation. When you collide with God's power, the object of transformation is not just *you*. Even though you are being hit, and you are being marked, and your true identity is being awakened, you step into the flow of something that was going on before you stepped onto the scene—and will continue when you are gone. He is the God who pours out His Spirit on *descendants* and *offspring*.

We miss the mark when we inappropriately elevate a single individual to a place of memorial without recognizing the *role* the person played in the continuing fulfillment of the purpose he or she served. We serve purpose, because we serve God. Remember, God is the God of Purpose. We are here to serve His purpose, not the other way around.

Consider King David. Scripture tells us that he *"had served God's purpose in his own generation…"* (Acts 13:36 NIV). Even the phrase, "served a purpose," carries the connotation that a purpose is beyond us. Purpose does not serve us; we serve it. We cater to it. We revolve our lives around purpose. We don't place demands on purpose. We don't dictate to purpose. Instead, we let it dictate to us; and as we serve God's purpose in our own generation, we play a vital part in the great unfolding agenda of God. You serve a multigenerational God. He is the God of Abraham, Isaac, and Jacob.

In serving God's purpose, we submit to His plan. Serving a purpose is not our invitation to celebrity status; serving a purpose is the call to lay everything at the feet of Jesus and say, "I'm in the King's service." The moment we take our eyes off the greater purpose of God and its multigenerational impact, we run into two dangers: 1) inappropriate focus on humanity, and 2) hindering the generational continuance of God's purposes.

When we take our eyes off the multigenerational nature of our purpose, we can mislead ourselves into believing that *we* are solely responsible for bringing our purpose to pass. This is both overwhelming and arrogance producing. It's overwhelming to believe that saving the entire world is on our shoulders, but it is likewise arrogance producing to assume that *we* have the ability to bring such a God-sized purpose to pass by ourselves.

We must be careful to always see ourselves in the context of the greater picture, the larger puzzle. Each person is interconnected pieces with other generations. When someone is divorced from the rightful place in the unfolding of a purpose, the person becomes elevated beyond appropriateness. The piece ends up receiving perverted recognition, for it is really the completed puzzle that solved the problem. The problem was incompletion; the process produced completion.

The process is beyond you, and it's beyond me. The process involves generations locking pieces to complete the puzzle. At one point,

IDENTITY

there was a puzzle that was missing pieces. However, as more and more pieces took their place in the puzzle, the purpose came to pass and was ultimately fulfilled. But think of how ridiculous it would be to assume that one piece, in and of itself, sufficiently completed the puzzle. This would be believing a lie and living in delusion. We play integral, interconnected parts in completing the most glorious puzzle conceivable—the puzzle of God's purpose being fulfilled in the earth.

> *You play an integral, interconnected part in completing the most glorious puzzle conceivable!*

God's great puzzle of purpose highlights two primary methods of interconnectedness between pieces. First, we are interconnected with each other in our present generation, recognizing what gifts, talents, abilities, and resources other people bring to the table in complementing who we are and likewise what we bring complementing who they are. Second, we recognize how our generation is vitally interconnected with future generations. In Psalm 145:4, we are given one of many examples throughout Scripture revealing God's vision for interconnecting generations.

This was God's purpose in colliding Elijah with Elisha. The puzzle did not conclude with Elijah. It would be tempting to gaze through the annals of history and fix our eyes on this man of power for his hour. Many of us do, in fact. We look at the life of someone God used powerfully and place an unhealthy amount of emphasis on *that one person,* when, in fact, we should be looking into his or her *purpose.* The purpose did not begin with that one person, and it does not end with that one person. While we honor the call of God upon someone, we must take it a step further and decipher the piece of the puzzle he or she served as in that generation. Why? This gives us clues to how the purpose will ultimately unfold.

IDENTITY

God's ministry of breakthrough, power, miracles, and cultural transformation did not conclude with Elijah; if anything, it increased in momentum when the mantle hit Elisha. The same is true for the work of God in this hour in your life. If you want to take your place as a carrier of God's purpose, you must recognize that purpose goes beyond yourself and beyond your generation.

 Reflection Questions

1. What is the "greater picture" of God's purpose for your life?

2. How does your purpose have many different dimensions?

3. Describe how you understand purpose to be multigenerational.

CHAPTER 5

FIND YOUR PLACE OF DEPOSIT

So Elijah went and found Elisha son of Shaphat plowing a field… (1 Kings 19:19 NLT).

MEETING THE CRITERIA FOR CARRYING PURPOSE

We just explored how purpose is much bigger than we might have imagined. In the same way that purpose did not start with us, it does not conclude with us. It is multigenerational. We briefly looked at the example of King

David, who *"had served God's purpose in his own generation"* (Acts 13:36 NIV). He recognized that purpose was bigger than his own piece of the puzzle, and simply served his uniquely assigned moment in history. Result? King David's life continued a momentum that ultimately birthed the Son of David, *Jesus Christ.*

In the same manner, Elijah sought to sow into a successor who would continue to carry his divinely assigned purpose. Going back in the story to where Elijah is discouraged after his Mount Carmel victory, the Lord informs him, *"I have reserved seven thousand in Israel, all whose knees have not bowed to Baal, and every mouth that has not kissed him"* (1 Kings 19:18). He was looking for soil to sow into, ready and fertile for the perpetuation of purpose.

It is important to note the principle here. Elijah was searching for a place of deposit and could find none. He had a mantle. He had experience. He had wisdom. He had revelation.

Find Your Place of Deposit

Elijah had so much to impart, so much to release, but it was reserved for specific ground.

Elijah's mantle was custom-sized for Elisha. Whether or not this is true in the literal sense, Elisha was the only one capable of wearing that mantle, for he was the designated place of deposit. The person of deposit is able to don the mantle. You see, none of the people Elijah had encountered or interacted with, up to this point, had met the criteria for the release of what he wanted to impart. Even though there were seven thousand in Israel who had not prostituted themselves with false gods, there was only one man suitable to be Elijah's spiritual successor. *Elisha* was Elijah's place of divine deposit. This is something we must learn to recognize if we are going to step into our purpose.

Don't waste your time trying to sow into unresponsive ground. It's got to be fertile. Listen, there is definitely a time for you to dig in, have resolve, and refuse to back up or back down. In these cases, your sowing is the very element God wants to use to supernaturally break up the fallowed ground (see Hosea 10:12). You need to exercise discernment and evaluate whether or not the ground is worthy of your seed.

What is your seed? It's your time. Your effort. Your passion. Your sweat. Your tears. Your intercessions. Your contending. Your laboring. When it comes time for you to sow and invest into someone else, identifying that person as a potential carrier and perpetuator of the purpose on your life, ensure that he or she is a suitable resting place for the deposit you carry. Otherwise, frustration will overwhelm the process.

Likewise, you need to prepare *your* heart to be fertile ground for what God wants to impart into your life. You really need to grasp both sides of this principle.

For the sake of this theme, you are Elisha. Got it? You are the one God wants to impart power into that will unlock your purpose. With that in mind, it's key to study how Elijah chose a successor to sow into. This shows us *who* God is looking for to collide with His power and release into divine destiny.

THE PRACTICAL SIDE OF SOWING

> *And he who reaps receives wages, and gathers fruit for eternal life, that both he who sows and he who reaps may rejoice together* (John 4:36).

Before we explore this principle any further, I want you to identify just how relatable it is to your life. I don't assume every person on the planet is a vagabond prophet like Elijah who just recently called fire down from Heaven. However, Elijah was a man marked by purpose. God had a purpose for Elijah in his generation prepared before the foundation of the world.

In the same way, the God of Elijah has marked you with purpose. He has fashioned you for destiny. We reviewed this in the opening pages. You're not a cosmic accident; you are the intricate handiwork of the God of Purpose. You have been placed in this moment, at this hour, in this season of history to fulfill your purpose in *your generation,* just as King David did.

What does this look like for the businessperson? The stay-at-home parent? The plumber? The accountant? The doctor? The coffee shop barista? The college student? The banker? Regardless what you are doing in life right now, you have been called to fulfill your purpose in your generation. Likewise, part of fulfilling your purpose is making an investment in other people and being one who is investable.

> *Part of fulfilling your purpose is making an investment in other people and being one who is investable.*

I want you to have eyes opened for the divine collisions in your life—not only for those who collide with you, but keep your eyes open to the people God brings into your life to collide with. You have something to release, and you have something to receive. Yes, you. I don't care what you're doing right now. I don't care if you are a multimillionaire or some broke college student living off noodles and peanut butter. Purpose is beyond your socioeconomic status. Purpose is not thwarted by the kind of house you currently live in. Purpose is not intimidated by your situation or circumstance. If you are a child of God, you carry the power of God—and that supernatural power awakens potential. You carry this power, and at any moment this same power can collide with you and unlock possibilities that your mind cannot even fathom. All it takes is a single moment. One encounter. A single meeting.

The key is sowing where your contribution is valued and appreciated. Right now, the context is you making investment into others. There will be times and places where what you bring is not appreciated, but it is something you *must do*. We can't go through life waiting to be appreciated before we do the right thing. That is not what I am talking about here.

IDENTITY

Our context is mentorship. We're talking about the people you make an investment in and pour your life into. It's about being on the lookout for those who carry your DNA. Sure, they might look differently, talk differently, act differently, smell differently, and dress differently. None of those externals matter when you see potential in that person. These are the people and environments where you are called to invest your pearls—the time, ability, gifting, talent, and wisdom of most precious value.

In the same way, I encourage you to be ready. Power is out there looking for you. Sowers are seeking those who carry the same DNA, same heartbeat, and same vision. You may look different, but that doesn't matter. If you are seed-ready ground, power's going to hit and awaken everything inside of you that needs to come out.

HOW TO IDENTIFY "SEED-READY" GROUND

*For he who sows to his flesh will of the flesh reap corruption, but he who **sows to the Spirit** will of the Spirit reap everlasting life* (Galatians 6:8).

Keep in mind, you cannot give your pearls to pigs (see Matthew 7:6). No matter how tired you are of carrying them, no matter how much you're ready to release them, you cannot take the things of God and give them to people who are not ready. There are those out there looking for seed-ready ground. What does this look like?

One of the key characteristics is a lifestyle of one who frequently sows *to the Spirit* (see Galatians 6:8). Their lifestyle is marked by spiritual investment. They are close with God—and you can see it. You see the fruit of their investment. Not everyone walks in this dimension, because not everyone stewards the seed he or she has received in the Spirit.

Think of all the believers out there. Yes, they are born again. Yes, they are washed in the blood. Yes, they have the Holy Ghost living inside them. Do you know how many people have this beyond priceless inheritance living inside them, and yet live like spiritual paupers? They live in spiritual poverty because they sow to the flesh. Their spirit was transformed when they were born again, but they still live like the world lives. They still operate and think and respond and behave like everyone else. Something happened in the core of their being, *but*, hear me, they are not sowing into it. They are not stewarding the seed of God in their own lives.

God planted a seed in their spirit when they came to Christ. That's the seed of His Spirit—the Holy Spirit. He's not looking to simply hang out, unbothered, in our spirits for 70, 80, 90, or 100 years. The Holy Spirit is a Person looking for cooperation. He's seeking ones who desire total invasion of every realm of life. He's waiting for the ones who will sow into the Spirit and reap for themselves transformed minds, healed emotions, and God-ward wills. This is where power is looking to invest and impart, into lives that recognize the power of investing in themselves. The ground must be spiritually ready. Are you?

Remember when Moses came down off the mountaintop with glory beams shooting out of his face (see Exodus 34:29-35)? He was ready to impart something to Israel that was not ready. They were sowing into the flesh. They received this glorious invitation from Jehovah, and what were they doing? Impatience brought them to idolatry. Moses comes down and finds them dancing naked around the golden calf and actually has to cover the glory that he was ready to release. Why? The people were not ready to receive on the level that he was ready to release. Do you see the parallel? For the power inside of you to release the potential in someone else, there must be a readiness on their end.

IDENTITY

> *Don't be caught dancing before the golden calf during your season of visitation.*

In the same way, for the power upon someone else to awaken your potential, you must be ready. For you to step into the things that God has purposed for your life, you must be prepared and be seed-ready ground. You must be ready in season and out of season. Don't be caught dancing before the golden calf during your season of visitation. Too many believers give up just before their moment, either because they cannot find fertile ground to release impartation, or because they have been patiently waiting to receive the mantle of Elisha and are losing heart. They are waiting for Moses to come down off the mountain—and are getting impatient.

I encourage you to be ready for your day of visitation. Be faithful. Continue plowing where God has you plowing right now. You don't know what it will look like, sound like, feel like, or smell like when power comes. God's timing is perfect, and it is sovereign. Your supernatural setup will come in His divine timing. Those catalysts that catapult you further and further into your purpose by awakening greater dimensions of untapped identity—they cannot be orchestrated by our scheming. They cannot be set up by our own human devices. In fact, when we insert ourselves into the process, we start tearing up the puzzle pieces.

Think of the other examples in Scripture. Jesus came onto the scene and said, *"I still have many things to say to you, but you cannot bear them now"* (John 16:12). There were certain realities that Jesus restrained Himself from sharing with the disciples because the soil was not yet ready for the impartation. It would only be ripe and ready upon the coming of the Holy Spirit.

WHEN THE STUDENT IS READY, THE TEACHER WILL APPEAR

And let us not grow weary while doing good, for in due season we shall reap if we do not lose heart (Galatians 6:9).

When the student is ready, the teacher will appear. This was certainly true for Elijah and Elisha, and it is likewise true for your life. You have to be ready to receive on the next level, and others have to be ready for your next level of impartation. By now you have probably noticed that all of us wear both hats at some point—teacher and student, Elijah and Elisha. All the while you are receiving from the teacher, you are releasing to students. All the while you are receiving as a student, you are releasing as a teacher. This is the process that Jesus described, *"Freely you have received, freely give"* (Matthew 10:8). As you receive more, more is able to flow through you.

When does the teacher appear on the scene? When the student is ready. You can't get the teacher to appear if the student isn't ready. The teacher has the power, and the student has the potential. Power needs to be released. It needs to express itself. It needs to reveal itself. However, potential needs to be ready in order for power to be recognized and have its full impact.

Two of the key characteristics of readiness are not growing weary and not losing heart, as Paul wrote in Galatians 6:9. The one who has been faithful in the former season demonstrates the character that will sustain him or her in the new season.

Consider Elijah again. He had no place to release this power. It felt like loneliness. Just think about the language he uses, *"I alone am left"* (1 Kings 19:10). He was in a wilderness, in a cave, and then on a mountain—in every place lonely and depressed. Why? Your loneliness and your agony come when you have something to release and no one is ready to receive it. He was looking for receive-ready ground where the seed of his impartation could find a resting place.

Take the conception process for example. Any creature will tell you there is nothing as laborious as trying to release a seed into a closed womb, a closed mind, an unreceptive audience. For example, I sow the Word of God as I preach. As much as a pastor, teacher, or preacher would love to help regulate the receptivity of the audience, such is not the case. Instead, the audience controls the flow of the Holy Spirit. No amount of hype and no amount of hoopla can fake a people ready to receive. When they're ready, they are ready. When they are not, they're not. Simple as that. We can press. We can push. We can sow and keep on sowing. Sometimes sheer perseverance starts to break up the ground, and then as one person starts getting hungry, others follow the lead.

Generally speaking, though, it is the recipient who controls the flow of the Holy Spirit in his or her life. Power is looking for recipients who are ready. Who are faithful. Who are hungry. Who are pressing in. Who are persevering through.

> **Power is looking for people who are ready, faithful, hungry, pressing in, persevering.**

I'm talking beyond preaching. Whatever you offer, wherever you are, and whatever your unique gifting is, for the sake of stewarding it well and not wanting to bang your head against the wall, find ready ground. *Be* the ready ground! Ask the Holy Spirit to bring you into a collision with those who are hungry and receptive—those who will receive and benefit from whatever you carry. It does not matter who you are or what your gift is.

If you're a businessperson, the principle is the same. Yes, there is a time for negotiation and salesmanship and marketing; but then there are people and companies that are just not ready to receive what you offer. Recognize

IDENTITY

this. Identify the relationships that are not ripe for your investment and discern the people who are ready for what you offer. You know what I'm talking about. There are people and situations that are just not ready for the glory that you bring.

On the other side, those who are receive-ready will actually draw the glory out of you. They will pull the revelation, potential, gifting, and anointing right out of you. This is what Elisha did for Elijah. Elisha was receive-ready, and Elijah—the teacher—showed up on the scene. There was a mutual recognition that each man was ready for what the other brought to the table.

There's another person inside you that the world has not seen yet. The time wasn't right before. You had to go through enough trouble, enough pain, enough agony, enough failure to get ready for this moment. But you're ready now. The teacher is appearing. The student is plowing. Remember, you are both the teacher and the student. Continue to sow; but at the same time, understand that to get to your next level, you need to be ready ground.

Look for a place to make a deposit of everything down inside you while waiting for the deposit that's coming your way. Yes, you're going to talk to some people about it, and they're not ready to even hear what you have to say. They're not ready for what you're discovering in these pages. Don't be frustrated when someone can't handle your glory, your gifting, your anointing, your revelation. Don't get upset because the ground is not ready yet. What's the solution? Find someone who has been praying and crying out for what you carry. Make the deposit in his life. Make the deposit in her life. And when the power of what you carry meets the potential inside that person, *something supernatural will happen.*

IDENTITY

Reflection Questions

1. What is the "place of deposit"?

2. Why is it so important for the ground to be *receive-ready?* How can you be that *receive-ready* ground?

3. What does the following statement mean to you: "When the student is ready, the teacher will appear"?

CHAPTER 6

Identifying Unrealized Potential

...Elisha the son of Shaphat, who was plowing with twelve yoke of oxen before him, and he was with the twelfth... (1 Kings 19:19).

UNSEEN POTENTIAL

Then Samuel took the horn of oil and anointed him in the midst of his brothers; and the Spirit of the Lord came upon David from that day forward... (1 Samuel 16:13).

IDENTITY

You carry a glory. There's something deep inside you that requires a meeting with God's power in order to be released. Your potential is awaiting activation. Elisha remains unrealized, unknown, obscure, and unseen until his meeting with Elijah.

This is what happened with King David. He was unseen—literally. While his brothers *looked* like royalty, it was the boy with the unseen character and unseen heart of worship and unseen victories over the bear and the lion to whom the prophet Samuel was drawn. He was the man for the mantle. God is looking to bring the unseen into the seen by using power to release your potential.

> **Something deep inside you requires a meeting with God's power to be released.**

Scripture is silent about Elisha *until* his meeting with Elijah. We don't get the privilege of learning his backstory. We're not told about his family life. We're left in the dark about his upbringing. Does this mean Elisha was unimportant before Elijah? No. Rather, the Bible gives us a glimpse into select moments where ordinary faithful men and women are launched out into their divine destinies. Before their collisions with power, they are still significant and valuable people. They simply carry unrealized and untapped potential. It's the intersection with power that draws out potential. It's the mantle that brings the unseen into the seen.

Scripture reveals example after example of those who experienced divine intersections with power, saw a release of potential, and ultimately stepped into the momentum of divine purpose.

Noah found favor in God's eyes. He had a family. He had a life. He had a concept of normal. And then God called him to build a boat that would ultimately save the planet. One intersection with power brought Noah out of the unseen into the seen.

IDENTITY

Abraham had a story. He had a homeland. *And then God called him out.* Power met Abraham's potential, and he began a journey toward stepping into his purpose. He left his homeland, dwelt in tents as a nomad, and ultimately had a child at an old age through a wife (who was long past the age of childbearing) who would go on to establish a heritage for generations to come.

Joseph was unseen until Pharaoh heard that Power enabled him to interpret dreams; he asked Joseph to interpret his own dream and, in turn, made Joseph prime minister of all Egypt.

Moses was an unseen shepherd in the wilderness until Power met him at the burning bush.

David was unseen until Power anointed him and said, *"You're* the King of Israel."

Jesus was even unseen until He was 30 years old, and Power opened the heavens and anointed Him.

When I say *Power,* I am referring to One Power. I'm not making reference to some ambiguous mysticism. I'm not talking about some otherworldly force or energy. I'm specifically addressing the power of the Most High God. Apart from His power and ability, we can do *nothing* (see John 15:5). In every situation we read about, there is a catalytic collision between God's supernatural power and a person's potential that brings them out of the unseen and into the seen.

> *A catalytic collision between God's supernatural power and your potential brings you out of the unseen and into the seen.*

Until First Kings 19:19, we do not meet Elisha. He is unseen potential. Elijah hears about him. God gives Elijah instruction on meeting him and what he will ultimately accomplish. However, until the collision with God's power, Elisha remains out of public view.

Do you feel unseen? Do you feel out of public view? Are you living in that place of obscurity right now? Listen, I realize there are people out there who *want to be seen*. No, they *need* to be seen. Their grand pursuit in life is self being seen. They depend on being noticed and recognized and celebrated and catered to in order to maintain their self-worth. That's not what I'm talking about here. You've lived satisfied in the secret place, but you recognize there is something inside you that *you offer* the world. It has not yet been revealed or released. It has nothing to do with you becoming a celebrity or a diva and has everything to do with you being receive-ready soil.

UNREALIZED POTENTIAL

Do not despise these small beginnings, for the Lord rejoices to see the work begin... (Zechariah 4:10 NLT).

Elisha was not only unseen potential, but he was also unrealized potential. As he plowed, surely he thought to himself, *I don't even know what I've got, but I know that doing what I'm*

Identifying Unrealized Potential

doing is not my destiny. Plowing was a day of small beginnings, but it was the plow that positioned him for the mantle. Elijah found Elisha while he was plowing.

Do you feel like Elisha—that you've got something, maybe you don't even know how to define it, but you know there is something more than what you are currently doing? That ache in the very core of your being, constantly reminding you that where you are cannot define *who* you are and for what you have been created. What you're doing right now cannot shape your vision and expectation of what you will be doing for the rest of your life. We are diligent in our present season, all the while recognizing that the potential inside us is not merely reserved for where we are *right now*, but it's unrealized.

In the same way we *realize* that we left our keys on the counter or we *realize* that we left our credit card at the restaurant, there are moments in your life when someone *realizes* the potential inside you. The person recognizes

IDENTITY

what's there—maybe you don't even see it, but someone does. Power does. When you realize something, it compels you to act. When Elijah realized the potential inside of Elisha, it caused him to pass by and toss his mantle upon him.

> *Unrealized potential always involves your supernatural capability.*

Before this incredible transference took place, Elisha had been plowing in the fields. He was working in the dimension of the natural, praying through the pain of working in this dimension of the natural. Unrealized potential always involves your supernatural capability. The things deep inside you are the very things that solve the deep needs and longings of humanity. This is beyond philanthropy, humanitarianism, and service. While these things are important, they are expressions of what's really inside you. There's supernatural potential burning in your natural frame. While there are gifts, talents,

Identifying Unrealized Potential

and abilities you have that are clear to everyone who sees you and knows you, Elijah calls out the deeper things. Power calls out the supernatural. Power commissions your ability to accomplish the impossible. Power summons you into the depths. Power invites you into the heights.

Elijah did not walk by Elisha, place his mantle upon him, and invite this plowman into a new dimension of natural work. In other words, Elijah did not summon Elisha into greater levels of plowing. Whether it was plowing in the field of a king, president, or prime minister, the natural act of plowing was not being called out of this man. In the same way, collisions with power, intersections with Elijahs, are not intended to simply upgrade what is already visible in your life. Elijah calls out the deeper things. He summons what's beyond the surface. He calls forth the things we didn't even know we had; and yet we somehow recognize that there is more to life than merely plowing a field.

Don't be satisfied settling for some type of natural upgrade and then calling it supernatural. Supernatural cannot be some term we assign to an extraordinary natural act that we are still capable of accomplishing through our own human effort, ingenuity, and skill. Many of us mistakenly assign the descriptive "supernatural" or "miraculous" to everything that requires just a little bit of extra sweat. I'm not demeaning the things we accomplish as human beings. God divinely knit us together with wisdom, skills, abilities, creative expression, fortitude, grit, gumption, and perseverance to do incredible things.

Humankind has built skyscrapers, gone to the moon, painted, sculpted, and crafted. Because of *how* humans are created, we are capable of creating. We celebrate the potential of humanity. We cheer on what we are capable of doing simply by how we were assembled through divine design. That's not what I want us to focus on right now.

I want to mess you up a little bit. I want to start a riot in your mind when it comes to your true potential. You have the potential to build a building of bricks and mortar, but you also have potential to transform the planet. You have the potential to fly to another galaxy, but also have the potential to change the culture to reflect your heavenly homeland. It might be unrealized right now, but it's there inside you. These realities are possibilities for you, even though they might be unrealized right now.

Unrealized potential causes us to ache to experience the supernatural power that ultimately unveils our true potential to the world.

LOVE THE ACHE AND KEEP PLOWING

> *Now may the Lord direct your hearts into the love of God and into the patience of Christ* (2 Thessalonians 3:5).

I encourage you to love the ache inside that reminds you of what's available, but currently not in operation. Why? Too many of us suppress this ache. We downplay the ache. There's a cry within us for more, but we don't know what to do with it. So many of us try to push mute on this ache for more. It's relentless; but the fact that it is unceasing until satisfied should cause us to celebrate what's available rather than settle for what is presently accessible.

> **There are realities available to you that you are not yet walking in.**

Plowing was Elisha's present-accessible reality. However, just because he was faithfully plowing did not mean he was ill-prepared for his moment of power. He was prepared because he did not run off and pursue some counterfeit version of what the deep of him surely longed for. I repeat, there are realities available to you that you are not yet walking in. Don't be disappointed that you are not walking in them… *yet*. Celebrate that they are available to you, and trust the God of Purpose to bring you into greater alignment with your supernatural purpose at His ordained time, through His methods.

Remember, purpose is recognized, experienced, and realized through those moments and meetings with power. Patience is absolutely required if we want to protect ourselves from settling for an inferior alternative.

This is what happens to those who are plowing—and grow tired. They become weary. They have not come to love the ache, but rather are desperate to silence its nagging noise. Day after day, night after night, as they plow in their place of present assignment, the ache within reminds them that another reality is available. Rather than trusting the God of Purpose and waiting for His power, we give up. We kick the ox. We toss the plow aside. We leave the field—running. Our quest becomes to silence the ache instead of waiting for God to satisfy it. As a result, we pursue counterfeit solutions to the ache for purpose.

Every attempt to satisfy our ache with second-rate pleasures will prolong our true launch into supernatural purpose. We try to access our potential, not through God's power, but through our own pursuits. Our pleasures. Our passions. These things will never ultimately silence the ache within.

Patience prepares us for the power that unleashes our potential. Just as patience protected Elisha from second-rate pursuits and prepared him for Elijah, so our patience actually helps enforce the character and integrity necessary to sustain the power that satisfies the ache. Elisha must be ready in order to receive Elijah's mantle. One key readiness factor is maintaining patience in the process of waiting, while also celebrating the ache that prophesies to us:

- "Elijah is coming!"

Identifying Unrealized Potential

- "Power is at hand!"
- "Things you didn't even know you had living inside you are getting ready to come forth!"

I don't believe it was a mistake that Elisha was found plowing, because plowing teaches you how to break up the hard places. Plowing teaches you that you cannot put a good seed in ground that is not prepared. Plowing is a process dedicated to readiness. Plowing teaches you seedtime and harvest, sowing and reaping. Plowing teaches you discipline and focus. Plowing teaches you how to follow. Plowing teaches you alignment.

> **Everything you have ever done has been in preparation for what you're about to do.**

There's a right kind of people for you to be aligned with and a wrong kind of people. The ache cries out for the right people and will never be satisfied with the wrong ones. It has to be lined up. Your relationships have to be lined up. You can't go out and plow just anywhere. There's a strategy. There's a structure. There's a purpose. There's a plan. There's a seed. You think you've been doing something that's beneath your anointing, but everything you have ever done has been getting you ready for what you're about to do.

Plowing prepared Elisha for Elijah. Whatever you're doing right now is preparing you for the next level. Everything you have ever done, every job you have ever worked. Everything that you thought was a deadbeat situation, every relationship you thought was beneath you—all of it was training for the promotion that is about to break forth in your life. Elijah's coming, and he's looking for a plowing Elisha.

Where will you be found on your day of visitation?

Identifying Unrealized Potential

Reflection Questions

1. What is unseen potential? Unrealized potential?

2. What is "the ache" inside of you? How should you respond to this ache?

3. What are the dangers of impatience while waiting for your moments and meetings with God's power?

CHAPTER 7

Unwrap the Gift of Exposure

Then Elijah...threw his mantle on him (1 Kings 19:19).

THE KEY THAT UNLOCKS POTENTIAL

Potential was plowing in the field, all the while waiting for something. Someone. A moment. A miracle. A collision. A release. A deposit. An impartation. An encounter. Potential was waiting for something, not knowing *what* that something would look like. The same is true for you. You carry unseen, unrealized

IDENTITY

potential. There is an ache inside you, constantly reminding you that *more* is available than you are currently seeing and experiencing. All of the factors are in place. You are following Elisha's example and faithfully plowing wherever you have been positioned. You are not looking to the right or the left. You're not allowing yourself to become distracted by other pursuits or counterfeit passions. With focus and fortitude you have made a resolution to move forward. You're not quitting. You're not stopping. You're not slowing down. You're not running off. You're not taking an indefinite coffee break. There's something *in* you waiting for something *out* there.

This brings us to the next step in the story of Elijah and Elisha. One day, Elisha looked up and saw Elijah. Potential looked up and saw power. What did power look like? The first expression power took was *exposure*. Exposure is a key that unlocks your purpose and identity. Power gives your identity exposure. Power can take obscurity, and in a moment, in a second, in an instant—through exposure—bring its potential into full view. Don't ever doubt the life-shaping power of one moment of exposure. You can't buy it. You can't manufacture it. You can't make it happen. Anything you strive after in the realm of exposure will always be a second-rate copy of the exposure released through a divine collision with power.

> *Power can take obscurity and in an instant–through exposure–bring its potential into full view.*

Elisha could have spent his entire life, as many people do, pursuing exposure for himself. Many of us run after something that, once we get it, we only experience its true ability in minor measure. Think about it. Here we are, plowing away, doing what God has called us to do and being where God has called us to be. Again, because of impatience and because we assume we can make something happen more effectively and efficiently than God, we run out and pursue exposure for ourselves.

I'm not saying all forms of pursued exposure are wrong. We need communications divisions. We need marketing campaigns. We need to get our message and materials and products and services out there. But there's a difference between marketing and manipulation. Do you see where I'm coming from? Marketing is stewardship of our services, gifts, talents, abilities, products, and resources, exposing them to people who will benefit from their use—while manipulation is trying to *become someone* through manufacturing exposure.

You can market all day long, that's fine. But when you know that, deep down inside, God has created you for something supernatural and significant, the worst thing you can do is run out and try to manufacture the exposure that will launch you into destiny. Again, exposure through marketing and communications is normal and natural; but the pursuit of exposure to actually fulfill your destiny, become who you were created to be, and step into your purpose is taking matters into your hands that they are not fit to carry.

Remember, only God can set up the exposure that is the key that unlocks your identity and propels you into your purpose.

THE GREAT GIFT THAT POWER DELIVERS

> *But I have raised you up for this very purpose, that I might show you My power and that My name might be proclaimed in all the earth* (Exodus 9:16 NIV).

One moment Elisha was a nobody out plowing fields. In the blink of an eye, he went from being a nobody to becoming successor to the greatest prophet in the land. Surely one of the greatest gifts you can give to anybody is exposure. God did this time after time. Again, reflect on Moses. One moment Moses was an obscure shepherd living in the wilderness;

the next, he is summoned to deliver a nation and demonstrate the power of God before the world's major superpower, Egypt.

One of the greatest gifts you can receive is exposure. Powerful people have influence, and influence is the foundation of exposure. Influence is what gives substance to exposure. Influence gives someone's exposure worth. Anybody can try to give you exposure. However, the only exposure that has the ability and power to unveil your true identity is exposure that comes from a source of value. Again, this source is influence. Only a person with influence has the ability to bring you valuable exposure.

Elijah had something of value to offer Elisha. There are people out there who think they are valuable; but in the end, they are just empty suits. They want influence. They crave power. They pursue recognition. Unfortunately, they are in it for themselves. They are me-centric. You don't want what they have, because they have nothing more than a façade. They might be able

Unwrap the Gift of Exposure

to dazzle you for a season, but when the dazzle wears off, they are void of anything raw or real. They are without substance, and it's substance that gives value to the exposure you receive.

Wait for the real; don't settle for the phony, the fake, or the flimflam. Impatience compels us to make some ridiculous moves. While waiting and plowing and waiting and plowing, we might see people who appear to "have it all." They look like they've got the power and prestige. You're looking at them, but they are not looking at you. In fact, nothing you do seems to be able to get their attention. This is not God restricting you; this is God preserving you. He is protecting you from falling prey to people who would invariably over-promise and under-deliver. Trust His divine timing. Wait for Elijah. Don't go chasing after every prophet who comes to town. Don't make just anyone your mentor. Don't try to manufacture a meeting with power, when in fact, the person you think offers exposure has nothing to offer you.

IDENTITY

Elijah was the real deal. He delivered the goods. He had what could push Elisha into the next dimension. The exposure Elijah offered carried significance and weight. He carried true greatness; and when God exposes you to greatness, even for the briefest of moments, if you have potential inside of you, when power passes by that potential, there is a cataclysmic explosion that takes place. Both will always recognize each other. Powerful people recognize potential in people, and people of potential know power when they see it. Whenever they pass by one another, potential says, "Now I get it! Now I see it! Now I understand it! Now I realize it!"

Then power says, "Do you know who you are, potential? You are standing on the verge. You think you're impressed with this. There's twice as much in you as there is in me, and when we meet...."

Elisha kept plowing and Elijah found him. Depending on what God has called you to do, your moments of exposure *will come*. Not everyone receives the same exposure because not everyone is designed to do the same thing. And remember, exposure comes, not by you chasing after it, but by you remaining faithful in your season, in your moment, in your job, in your family, in your project, in your everyday life. Power that brings exposure is attracted to the faithful, for it is the faithful who can survive the pressure and weight of exposure.

ARE YOU READY FOR YOUR MOMENT?

"Now therefore, fear the Lord, serve Him in sincerity and in truth..." (Joshua 24:14).

Faithful plowing reveals a heart that is ripe and ready for an encounter with power. Many people live in the waiting room, not because of God's unwillingness to promote, but because of their unwillingness to be faithful in their current life situation. Faithfulness and integrity are key qualities to promotion through exposure.

God is seeking those who serve Him in *sincerity and truth*. He's looking for those who are hungry for the next level, but also understand that the key to stepping into that level is being faithful where they are.

> **Faithfulness and integrity are key qualities to promotion through exposure.**

Exposure is the greatest of blessings for the one who carries potential and stewards it well through a lifestyle of steadfastness, faithfulness, and integrity. This person is poised for the touch of power that releases the exposure needed for living in the next dimension. However, exposure can bring complete destruction and untold ruin to the life not ready for everything that accompanies it. God denies exposure for the sake of protection, not restriction. Anything that would hinder us from walking into our purpose is a red flag as far as Heaven is concerned.

Many have been crushed by preseason promotion. They have pushed their way through the crowd, and instead of waiting for divine timing, they knocked down the door and did what they could in order to secure the object of their desire. A promotion, a blessing, or a breakthrough received before we are ready for it can crush us under its weight. This is not to say God expects perfection from those He blesses. Time after time, it's His blessings that invite us into new levels of maturity and development. At the same time, I am not referring to a deliverance from bondage or a healing from a disease right now. I am talking about a promotion that takes you into a new level, a new dimension, and a new season of life.

If you don't have what it takes to stand strong in your new season, then the very thing that was meant for your blessing, *in due season*, could harm or even destroy you preseason. This is why patience cannot be emphasized enough. Elisha did not find Elijah preseason. That mantle could have killed him before that divine moment. The responsibility would have been too much for him. He needed to plow more. He needed to learn the value of hard work, time management, and discipline. Elisha was not perfect when Elijah found him, but he was prepared. He was ready for his moment.

Are you ready for yours?

I assure you, as you continue to faithfully plow in this season, God Almighty is faithfully preparing you for the next. Every moment you continue in the natural, faithfully plowing, faithfully working, faithfully going to school, faithfully serving, something supernatural is taking place behind the veil. Your lifestyle of faithfulness attracts the gaze of Heaven. Every moment you stick to the plowing process, you are becoming more and more fit for your meeting of power and moment of exposure.

You don't even know what's going on inside you. You are gloriously clueless to what the Creator is working on and weaving behind the scenes. You may feel like you're sitting in the back. You might feel unnoticed and unrecognized. You may even feel like saying, "If I have to plow one more day, one more time, one more moment, I'm gonna throw that thing in the ditch." Yet there is something pushing you. Someone is compelling you to keep going. Keep plowing. Keep reading. Keep studying. Keep working. Keep giving. It doesn't matter if no one knows your name. You may have no recognition whatsoever.

The truth is, you are potential ready for action. There's potential energy inside you just waiting for that push of kinetic power. You are stationary until that one bump, one push, or one spark comes along and launches you right into the next dimension.

Your moment is at hand. That's why you can't be satisfied. That's why you can't sit back and look around. You are potential waiting for power to release you into your full identity and purpose. You're just waiting for the hookup. And as soon as you get that hookup, you're going to go up. You're next in line for the hookup. You are not forgotten. You are not on some shelf somewhere. The eyes of the Lord God are upon you. His favor surrounds you. His glory is within you. His power is around you.

You've been plowing in the field waiting for the right time, waiting to be in the right place, and waiting for the right mantle to pass over you. Get ready. Power is coming that will expose your true identity and unlock your purpose.

Reflection Questions

1. How is exposure valuable when it comes to releasing your potential?
2. Is it possible to pursue false exposure?
3. What happens if you experience exposure before you are ready for your "moment?" Why would God deny exposure to you?

Final Thoughts

How is it possible that people can go through their entire lifetimes, desperately searching for significance and purpose, and yet, never feel as though they found it? Simple. Many reach the end of their lives with regret and disappointment because of how much time and energy they invested trying to be *someone else*.

I want things to be different for you. Page after page of *Identity* has been crafted with one purpose: to remind you of who *you are*.

You are the *only* you that there will ever be. *Ever.* Throughout history, *you* are unique.

IDENTITY

You are one of a kind!

No one else can do things just like you.

No one else can process and understand like you.

You may notice slight similarities between you and others, but believe me—you are an original.

For every original man and woman that God created, there is an original purpose for his and her life.

Others might come alongside to help you along the journey. People might mentor you, sowing into your personal development. God might even bring an "Elijah" figure into your life who has already gone where you are going, and can give you a very unique vantage point on walking out your purpose. Leaders may lay hands on you and release impartation.

Celebrate all of these as the catalysts they are meant to be, while also recognizing that no person, no leader, no act of impartation, or no mentor has the ability to fulfill your purpose for you. Only you have that power! God created you unique so that, through you, He could boldly express a facet of His character that no one else in history could! Think of it. Who you are reflects Creator God to the world in a way that no one else *ever could*—past, present, or future. The more you step into your purpose, the more brightly you will radiate God's nature.

Get ready. As you discover who you really are, you will *never* want to be someone else again!

BONUS MATERIAL

Intro, Chapter One of

Cora Jakes Coleman's

Faithing It

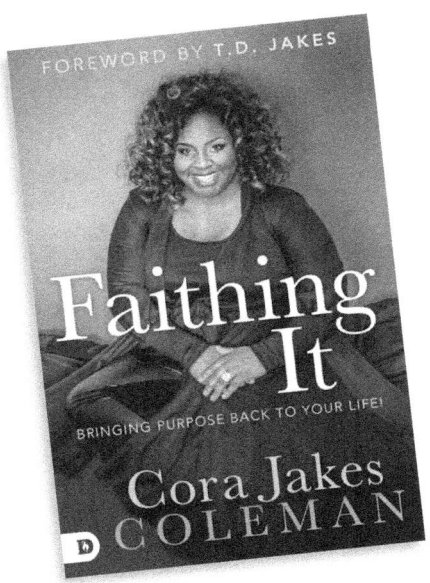

Introduction

"Faithing it." What does that mean? It means that in order to get through our problems and bypass our circumstances, we must fight with faith—and without a faith fight there cannot be a win. Faith is obtained by God! If we choose to speak faith and fight obstacles with our faith, we cannot lose.

Are you in a struggle right now? I want you to know that you are not alone. God has you in His hand! You *will* make it, and I'm here to tell you that there is not just one way to win, there are several ways to win.

I wrote this book because I love you, and I do not want you to feel alone or be alone. I want to be clear. Just because my earthly father is known as "the world's bishop," that doesn't mean that I am above you. I am coming to you as a friend and sister to encourage you to leap into your dream, purpose, and promise. My hope is that you walk away with a better understanding of who you are and what your struggles mean in connection to your ultimate destiny.

> *Without a faith fight there*
> *cannot be a win.*

Before we begin this journey together, I want to tell you a story that I tell to audiences everywhere I speak. This story is really what led me to faithing it. This story is why I'm telling you to fight with faith for your purpose.

The "Accident"

I was twenty-two years old, engaged to the most wonderful man in the world, and thoroughly enjoying my work as a nanny and babysitter. One evening before going off to work, I told my mother that my hips and back hurt so badly, but I wasn't sure why.

That night on the way home from the babysitting job, I was driving and talking to my fiancé on the speaker phone when my green arrow light came up to turn left. So I began to turn, and suddenly I looked up to headlights coming directly at me. I immediately prayed, "God get me out of this." The truck rammed into me going 40 mph. My air bag burst in my face and glass shattered everywhere. My car caved in on me.

I was scared. This was the worst car accident I had ever been in. I remembered one thing. I prayed God would get me out of this. I believed God would get me out of this when the collision ended. I opened my eyes. My coat was burned from the airbag, and all I could hear was, "She's dead! She has to be dead!" The fireman came running to my car and I opened my car and stood up—without a visible bruise or scratch—nothing. I was just sore.

I didn't go to the emergency room that night. I went home that night asking God why me? Why would you cause me to go through that? What was the purpose of this? I woke up very sore the next day. My mother took me to the doctor.

During the CAT scan at the doctor's office, they found a 7 cm cyst on one ovary and a 9 cm cyst on my other ovary. The doctor told me that I was days away from my fallopian tubes twisting and shutting down my reproductive system.

Why Me, God?

I was stunned. All I ever wanted to be was a mother. Everything that I dreamed about, everything I hoped for would have been impossible had it not been for a car hitting me at 40 mph. If the devil had his way I would have been dead, and everything that would allow me to produce would have been dead.

You may not know the why, but sometimes the hard things happen to us because we are being saved from the enemy destroying our ability to produce. Whether spiritual or natural, the enemy is after your seed. You may have just been hit hard and you may be in pain but all of this is leading to your salvation.

God saved me in a unique way because God is a unique God and He has to orchestrate things accordingly. Had I not gone through the hurt, the soreness, and later the surgery I would have been in a lot of trouble. Later, the surgeon discovered that one of the cysts was much larger than they originally thought, and because of that I would have to lose one of my fallopian tubes and one of my ovaries.

One hit by a car led to me to discovering two cysts, the loss of an ovary, the loss of a fallopian tube, and a news flash from the doctor that it wasn't probable for me to get pregnant without going through in-vitro fertilization. Needless to say, I was devastated by the news. I saw the pain of the process, and I was hurt by the facts in front of me. I wanted to live in the "Why Me God?", but had I not gone through all that I wouldn't have gotten to the great rewards of my life.

What's Your Story?

So what's your story? Do you have unanswered questions about the circumstances in your life? Are you wondering when your rewards are coming?

I want to invite you right now to join me in faithing it—fighting with your faith to produce purpose. If you decide to faith it, the enemy will not control your story, your win, or your life. This is *your* time to move forward with zeal, tenacity, and determination. This book is going to inspire you to believe God, and push you to stretch and develop the fighter in you.

Introduction

Are you ready to stand up and faith it with me? I want you to know that I believe God's best is just ahead for both of us. Let's talk.

CHAPTER
ONE

You Are God's Book— Respect the Process

> *You saw me before I was born. Every day of my life was recorded in your book. Every moment was laid out before a single day had passed.*
> —Psalm 139:16 NLT

God is the author of your story! Every good story has a multi-dimensional character that experiences inner struggles, outer conflicts, and a satisfying "aha moment" where everything finally comes together for that character. You can't go to a bookstore, pick up a book, tear out the happy parts that you like, and then move on. If you pick up that book and you want those eight pages that you like, then you will have to buy all the other pages. And to live a successful life in all the other chapters of your book, you're going to need to faith it to the last page! God is crafting a marvelous book about each one of us, and in order to get to complete wholeness we must first understand our life is a series of processes all built to create us into the person God wants us to be. Don't worry! Your "aha moment" is on the way!

I started dating my (now) husband Brandon six years ago and boy we were head over heels in love! When you are that in love you have the tendency to want to move really quickly. Whenever we would feel the "urge" to move quickly,

Brandon would look at me and say, "We have to respect the process." At the time, though, it was so difficult. Although I knew what he meant, I had to patiently realize that there was a process that had to be implanted in order for us to get to our ultimate goal. We loved each other and we were grown, but it was not a time for "urgencies" and we had to respect the process. I had to grow more, and he did too.

Don't worry!
Your "aha moment" is on the way!

All great things come with a process. Was it hard for Brandon and me? Indeed! At first it was very hard, and then it became easy as God grew and matured us. We faced trials for sure and gained major perseverance but at the end of the day it was our respect for our process that got us to our goal. Really, in all honesty, trusting God is the process. Allowing Him to lead you is the ultimate maturity.

You Can't Skip the Process

You have to understand that "the process" is a normal way of life. When you think about the basic things of life, there's a process. When you are getting ready to cook for your family you pick something out, and then you build a grocery list, and then you have to go get the groceries, and preheat ovens, and prepare your meal. The meal cannot come forth without a process, and if you do not go through the process your family will be hungry. Even when you are tired, working, and things are going crazy, you have to cook and you have to go to the grocery store. You cannot skip the process. No matter how easy the meal is, you cannot skip the process to get there.

When you are crying out to God for Him to do something and it does not come through, you wonder, Lord, why are you blessing everyone else connected to me, but not blessing me? It is in that very moment in the middle of your WHY that God is telling you respect the process—trust Me. It is in your maturity and completeness where you realize God is for you, and what He said He would fulfill. He will, but you must trust Him.

Our lives are living testaments of several processes both big and small. In our relationships of life there is a process. The point is, you can't run away from the process. You have to face it. If you want to be a wife, a husband, or even someone's significant other you have to go through a process.

Being in a relationship you will have obstacles, ups and downs, but it's all a process in order to get you to your promise. God is asking you to face your process, face your trials, and when you can believe God in the midst of your trial then, and only then, can you not lack anything. Your promise is in your problems. Those problems are there so you do not lack anything. God wants you to mature and become complete. Now when we look at "complete" I know that can be confusing, but it means that He wants you to be whole—He wants you to be full. The book of James tells us about the process that brings us to maturity:

> *Consider it pure joy, my brothers and sisters, whenever you face trials of many kinds, because you know that the testing of your faith produces perseverance. Let perseverance finish its work so that you may be mature and complete, not lacking anything* (James 1:2-4 NIV).

*It's all a process in order to
get you to your promise.*

Perseverance as defined on Google is "steadfastness in doing something despite difficulty or delay in achieving success." James chapter one tells us that the testing of our faith will bring perseverance. So God was simply saying yes we will face trials, and yes it is going to be hard. But the good news is that our current hardship is going to develop steadfastness in whatever we do, despite difficulty or delay in our leap of faith.

Are you looking for purpose? Chances are, your purpose and your plan are right there in your face. Let me explain how this happened to me.

The Chapter in My Book that I Didn't Like

As I entered adulthood, I felt pretty steady and secure. I had realized one dream of working with children, and God loved me enough to allow me to meet the love of my life—an amazing man and artist, Brandon Coleman a.k.a. Skii (Sky) Ventura, and my life as far as I knew it was going great. Then I hit another obstacle. I mentioned in the introduction to this book the accident that I was in when Brandon and I were engaged to be married. Since that time, I've been in the fight of my life. I am currently dealing with the diagnosis that I will not get pregnant without fertility treatments due to PCOS (Polycystic Ovarian Syndrome). This very diagnosis is one of the reasons why I wrote this book.

After hearing such horrible news, right when we were ready to marry and start a family, I was heartbroken. I didn't like this chapter in my book at all! Yet again, here I was going through "everything that a young woman goes through." For years, I dreamed of becoming a mother, not to mention the fact that I had "mothered" countless children in my day care work and as the Children's Ministry Director of the Potters House of Dallas. Now to hear I would not have children—I was disappointed beyond belief. BUT I did not let that stop me from trying, preparing, and getting ready to become a mother.

Often we let what the world says detour us from our desire and from what God said would happen. Then instead of even trying, we stop fighting altogether. Not me! I shook myself off and I looked for ways to make my dream come true. I became a mom to my beautiful daughter through adoption. I experienced the miracle of choosing my beautiful daughter. You don't have to birth a child in order to be a mom. With that being said, never make a back-up plan for what God promised you. Keep the faith in the promise! When I was a little girl, I had a dream one night of being a mom to a son. I am holding on to the promise of my son from God, and I won't and can't stop faithing it until it comes to fruition.

You have to make up your mind to fight for your promise! The power is in your fight, so FIGHT FOR IT! You can do it.

Faithing It with Perseverance

God is developing your purpose through your trial, and it's likely that you are currently in the process—meaning a series of actions or steps taken in order to achieve a particular end. The process of life cannot come without perseverance. Beware! You can lose your promise when you do not match the two together. It is important that whatever you go through in life that you go through it with perseverance while faithing it for your promise.

Whenever I think of perseverance, I think of my favorite story in the Bible—Job (pronounced Jobe). Maybe you've heard someone say, "It's been a Job day." That means, "I am having an incredibly difficult day and everything that could go wrong, did go wrong!" Job was a man of God and an entire book of the Bible is named after Job and is dedicated to his story. Let me tell you a little bit about Job!

You see, the Bible says Job was an upright man, and, because of the greatness that he sought, he was chosen to go through great trials. How crazy is it that? We get chosen to go through great trials when we are Christians?

Faithing It

What sense does that make to go through problems when you are a child of the King? What if I told you that you were chosen to go through trials because you are a child of the King seeking righteousness, and the enemy wants to destroy your promise and your ability to prosper?

Here's how it went down. Satan went to God in heaven to accuse the people on earth. (Satan still accuses God's people, even today.) When satan accused the people living on the earth during Job's day, God said to satan, "Have you considered my servant Job?"

Satan replied, "No wonder Job's so righteous. Look at that hedge of protection you've put around him! Take down that hedge and I'll get him to curse you" (see Job 1:8–11).

God allowed satan a limited access to Job, and Job lost everything but his life. He got sick, he was shaken, he was broken, yet he never once cursed God—although he did curse himself. There will be times in life when you wonder where God is, and He is standing right there, but He is taking you through the process in order to bless you. You must understand that the enemy is not hitting you without God's permission. You need to know that the importance of Job's story is that the enemy had to go before God before even touching Job. Your circumstance does not come without granted approval from the throne. It is also important to note that the enemy is not a creator—he is an imitator. If he attacked Job, then he will attack us, too. Whatever the enemy presents to you is just a reconstructed situation that he has used before.

Job's friends thought he was crazy. His wife turned against him and even tempted him to sin! She said, "Why don't you just curse God and die?" What a test! But Job still trusted God while he was in his process, and he never stopped believing in God.

You are designed by God to persevere. You are designed to face trials because you need them in order to get to the promise. Before you can get to what God has for you, you will have to face adversity.

Whatever the enemy presents to you is just a reconstructed situation that he has used before.

Processes are not easy. Think about all of the conflict and struggles a main character goes through in a novel or even a movie. Those intense struggles make the "aha moment" even better! So keep faithing it, no matter where you are in your process.

From the Process to the Promise

Sometimes we have to process our mind, friends, and family before we can get to our promise. The overall point is this:. Are you willing to go through the process in order to get to the thing God wants for you? Even if it means losing everything in order to gain more in the end?

Philippians 3:8 says, "Yet indeed I also count all things loss for the excellence of the knowledge of Christ Jesus my Lord, for whom I have suffered the loss of all things, and count them as rubbish, that I may gain Christ" (NKJV).

You see, there is much to gain! Not only will you obtain God's promises for your life, but you walk out of your process knowing Jesus!

Let's consider Jesus. Jesus was a carpenter. He created things, and He was a builder. Jesus was God in the flesh, and it's only natural that we will go through processes in life simply because Jesus was a builder. He was a carpenter, and carpenters know more than most that there is a process in everything that you want to create. They understand that you cannot make something without a process.

Step out of who you think you are and who people think you are and begin to walk in what God spoke over you. And just in case you did not know who God said you are then you need to just walk in the simple fact that you are a child of the King of Kings. You are a child of a carpenter, and He is building you into something beautiful. Molded and created in His perfect image, you can walk in the fact that you are called to be great.

I believe that fighting and faith go hand in hand. That's what gets us through these obstacles—our ability to stand before the mountain with faith and a fight and command the mountain to move. It WILL move!

Every super hero has a villain, and every hero has a backstory.

God is molding you to be great. He is molding you to overcome. He is molding you into completion and maturity. You are not forgotten. You are worthy of your dreams and hopes. You are not being punished; you are being processed. You deserve to gain all God has for you. Do not limit yourself because the storms are raging, but look at the storm and say, "I will trust you Lord." If you were not meant to be anything, you would not have trials to face. If you were not meant to be strong and great then you would need no molding.

I wrote this book because I believe in you. As your sister in Christ, I am here to faith it

Faithing It

with you so we can rise up together against the enemy and break his chains!

You are God's book, and right now, today, you are living out a page in that book. Is today's page overwhelming you? Do you feel alone in this chapter of your life? As your sister and friend I want to tell you that it is through your hurt that you become a hero. Every super hero has a villain, and every hero has a backstory. Will you let me pray for you right now?

> *I pray that God give you the grace to endure the pain of the process. I pray that God open your eyes to see the people who are for you and the people who are not. I pray that God allow you to embrace this in a new way where you understand that your storms have been meant to make you grow stronger. I*

pray that God ignite the purpose and gifting inside of you that you might be able to go after your purpose with everything that you have. I pray that faith be your encourager, that faith be your pusher, that faith be your strength, and that you begin to become a faither. I pray that you take on this challenge to become better than who you are, that you do not look behind you, and that you do not let the enemy keep you bound in the past, but that you challenge yourself to be even better than who you think you are supposed to be. I pray that you give God the ability to do great things in you. I pray you get something out of this journey, and that you understand that I am here for you, I am faithing with you, and trust me, we are going to win and I pray you know that.

BONUS MATERIAL

A Selection from

STRENGTH
FOR EVERY
MOMENT

Day 1
I Can Do All Things

I can do all things through Christ who strengthens me (Philippians 4:13).

DECEPTION is a trap and stronghold that ensnares many, especially those not content with their own present state in life. The Bible instructs us that we must learn to be content in whatever state we find ourselves. The apostle Paul learned that lesson well: "*...for I have learned, in whatsoever state I am, therewith to be content*" (Phil. 4:11 KJV).

This is not to imply that we should be satisfied with being bound by the devil or be content with complacency and mediocrity, thus not fulfilling the call of God on our lives. Not at all. We are to work to improve ourselves while at the same time remaining totally dependent on God.

STRENGTH FOR EVERY MOMENT

Self-sufficiency means to be "sufficient in oneself" and not putting your faith in God's assistance. Contentment, on the other hand, is to know with certainty and absolute firm conviction that God is able to meet your every need; Jehovah is your all-sufficiency. Contentment means that you are aware that you don't covet another person's position, property, possessions, or personality. Why? Because you know and are assured that all you presently have and all that you are today is more than enough in the hands of God. Whatever you need to do to fulfill God's purpose you can do, not in your own strength, but through the strength and power of Christ that dwells within your innermost being.

The apostle Paul said:

I know how to be abased, and I know how to abound. Everywhere and in all things I have learned both to be full and to be hungry, both to abound and to suffer need. I can do all things through Christ who strengthens me (Phil. 4:12-13).

Day 1

CONSIDERATIONS

1. Like Paul, have you learned to be content in your present state in life? Why or why not? What possible ways are you being deceived into discontentment?

   _____

   _____

   _____

2. In your own words, define the difference between being content and being complacent. Are you doing all you can do to fulfill the call of God in your life?

   _____

   _____

3. List five things that you think of when you consider the word "contentment." Are those things present in your life? How can you improve your contentment level?

_____

_____

_____

_____

4. Contentment means that you don't covet another person's position, property, possessions, or personality. Was there a time (or times) when you were aware of coveting another's position, property, possessions, or personality? Have you completely abandoned those thoughts and desires? Why or why not?

_____

_____

_____

Day 1

5. What recent steps have you taken to fulfill God's purpose for you? What additional steps can you take today, tomorrow?

   _____
   _____
   _____
   _____

STRENGTH FOR EVERY MOMENT

MEDITATION

I know how to be abased, and I know how to abound. Everywhere and in all things I have learned both to be full and to be hungry, both to abound and to suffer need. I can do all things through Christ who strengthens me (Philippians 4:12-13).

Do you trust Christ to give you strength to do *all* things?

Day 2
Renew Your Strength

He gives power to the weak, and to those who have no might He increases strength. Even the youths shall faint and be weary, and the young men shall utterly fall, but those who wait on the Lord shall **renew their strength***; they shall mount up with wings like eagles, they shall run and not be weary, they shall walk and not faint* (Isaiah 40:29-31).

When your pity party is over and you are ready for His help, God will say, "Don't you know? Have you not heard Who I am—the everlasting God? I am the Creator of the universe. I am not a child; I am not a school boy—I am God. Who do you think you're fooling? I'm God. I hold your breath in My hands. I created your body. I heat your blood just hot enough to keep you alive but not so hot that you die. Who else do you allow to control your life? If it is not Me, then who? I love you. I created you in My image. I am that I am."

What more does the Lord have to do or say to show you He loves you? Don't let satan continue to fool you into thinking that God has forsaken you.

Stop doing things that you know you don't have any business doing. Repent and confess your sins instead of spending your time pointing out the sins of everyone else. Admit that you have fallen so that your healing may begin.

Day 2

CONSIDERATIONS

1. Have you hosted your own pity party lately? Did you invite others? How do you feel after the party is over? Refreshed or defeated?

   _____

   _____

   _____

2. Do you believe that God is the great "I am"? What does that title or term mean to you? Define the great "I am" in two to three sentences.

   _____

   _____

   _____

   _____

3. Think of 10 ways that the Lord helps you through each day. Write them down and thank Him for each one.

_____

_____

_____

_____

_____

4. Has satan fooled you into thinking that God has forsaken you? What can you do to keep satan from fooling you?

_____

_____

5. Most people tend to judge others but don't realize the things wrong in their own lives. The next time you start to say something about another, stop first and think about issues in your own life that need to be addressed.

Day 2

MEDITATION

He gives power to the weak, and to those who have no might He increases strength. Even the youths shall faint and be weary, and the young men shall utterly fall, but those who wait on the Lord shall **renew their strength**; *they shall mount up with wings like eagles, they shall run and not be weary, they shall walk and not faint* (Isaiah 40:29-31).

How many times have you felt faint and weak, but the Lord renewed your strength and you went on to accomplish your goal?

Day 3
My Understanding Returned

And at the end of the time I, Nebuchadnezzar, lifted my eyes to Heaven, and **my understanding returned** *to me; and I blessed the Most High and praised and honored Him who lives forever.... At the same time my reason returned to me, and for the glory of my kingdom, my honor and splendor returned to me. My counselors and nobles resorted to me, I was restored to my kingdom, and excellent majesty was added to me. Now I, Nebuchadnezzar, praise and extol and honor the King of Heaven, all of whose works are truth, and His ways justice. And those who walk in pride He is able to put down* (Daniel 4:34,36-37).

Repentance was the key to Nebuchadnezzar's healing and deliverance.

To fall is bad enough, but to fall and not cry out for help, refusing to repent for your sin, is worse than the fall itself. Some people are so full of pride and consumed with their own self-sufficiency that they think, "If I can't get up myself, I won't let anyone help me."

Maybe you are ashamed to let anyone know that you have fallen because you don't want them to think less of you. Is your image so important that you're willing to continue in your pitiful fallen state? Are you so deceived that you will not acknowledge that you have sinned? Stop being so proud. After all, isn't that what caused you to fall in the first place?

Pride is dangerous because it forces you to lie needlessly in a helpless state for days—and sometimes years. If you had asked for help immediately, you could have gotten up and gone on with your life.

Day 3

CONSIDERATIONS

1. *Repent* means to feel remorse, self-reproach, and to feel such regret for past conduct as to change one's mind regarding it. It also means to make a change for the better as a result of contrition for one's sins. Have you repented of conduct that you know God would not approve?

   _____

   _____

2. All are guilty of prideful thoughts and actions from time to time. Think of a time that you know pride was the root of the problem. Did you dig it out and destroy it? If not, do so soon.

   _____

   _____

3. Is it hard for you to ask others or God for help?

   _____

   Why? _____

   _____

   _____

4. After you ask God for help, how do you feel? Giving your problems to Him totally brings a peace that passes all understanding. Do you know that?

   _____

   _____

   _____

   _____

5. Going on with your life after a fall or failure actually empowers you to do greater things. What greater thing can you begin today?

   _____

   _____

Day 3

MEDITATION

*And at the end of the time I, Nebuchadnezzar, lifted my eyes to Heaven, and **my understanding returned** to me; and I blessed the Most High and praised and honored Him who lives forever.... At the same time my reason returned to me, and for the glory of my kingdom, my honor and splendor returned to me. My counselors and nobles resorted to me, I was restored to my kingdom, and excellent majesty was added to me. Now I, Nebuchadnezzar, praise and extol and honor the King of Heaven, all of whose works are truth, and His ways justice. And those who walk in pride He is able to put down* (Daniel 4:34, 36-37).

Have you lost your understanding of the Most High? Open your ears, mind, and heart and allow your understanding and your reasoning to welcome Him into your entire being.

JOIN *the* CLUB

As a member of the **Love to Read Club,** receive exclusive offers for FREE, 99¢ and $1.99 e-books* every week. Plus, get the **latest news** about upcoming releases from **top authors** like...

T.D. Jakes, Bill Johnson, Cindy Trimm, Jim Stovall, Beni Johnson, Myles Munroe, *and more!*

JOIN NOW at *destinyimage.com/freebooks*

SHARE *this* BOOK

Don't let the impact of this book end with you! *Get a discount when you order 3 or more books.*

CALL TO ORDER
1-888-987-7033

destinyimage.com  1-800-722-6774

CPSIA information can be obtained
at www.ICGtesting.com
Printed in the USA
LVHW081440100520
655301LV00019B/1106